"Publish this Work ("The Poem of the Man-God ") as it is. It is not necessary to give any opinion about its origin or whether it can be extraordinary or not. Whoever reads it, will understand"

His Holiness Pope Pius XII,
February 26, 1948.

Code Of Canon Law

Canon 66 "The Christian economy, therefore, since it is the new and definitive Covenant, will never pass away; and no new public revelation is to be expected before the glorious manifestation of our Lord Jesus Christ." Yet even if Revelation is already complete, it has not been made completely explicit; it remains for Christian faith gradually to grasp its full significance over the course of the centuries.

Canon 67 Throughout the ages, there have been so-called "private" revelations, some of which have been recognized by the authority of the Church. They do not belong, however, to the deposit of faith. It is not their role to improve or complete Christ's definitive Revelation, but to help live more fully by it in a certain period of history. Guided by the Magisterium of the Church, the sensus fidelium knows how to discern and welcome in these revelations whatever constitutes an authentic call of Christ or his saints to the Church.

Christian faith cannot accept "revelations" that claim to surpass or correct the Revelation of which Christ is the fulfilment, as is the case in certain non-Christian religions and also in certain recent sects which base themselves on such "revelations."

The Full Of Grace:
The Early Years.
The Merit.
Joseph's Passion.
The Blue Angel.
The Boyhood Of Jesus.

Follow Me:
Treasure With 7 Names
Where There Are Thorns, There Also Will Be Roses
For Love That Perseveres
The Apostolic College
The Decalogue

The Chronicles Of Jesus & Judas Iscariot:
I See You As You Are
Those Who Are Marked
Jesus Weeps

Lazarus:
That Beautiful Blonde
Flowers Of Bounty

Claudia Procula:
Do You Love The Nazarene?
The Caprice Of Court Morals

Christian Tenets:
On Reincarnation

Mary Of Magdala:
Ah! My Beloved! I Reached You At Last!

Lamb Books
Illustrated adaptations for the whole family

LAMB BOOKS

Published by Lamb Books, 2 Dalkeith Court, 45 Vincent Street, London SW1P 4HH;

UK, USA, FR, IT, SP, DE

www.lambbooks.org

First published by Lamb Books 2013
This edition
001

Text copyright @ Lamb Books Nominee, 2013

Illustrations copyright @ Lamb Books, 2013
The moral right of the author and illustrator has been asserted
All rights reserved

The author and publisher are grateful to the Centro Editoriale Valtoriano in Italy for Permission to quote from the Poem of the Man- God by Maria Valtorta, by Valtorta Publishing

Set in Bookman Old Style R

Printed and bound by CPI Group (UK) Ltd, Croydon, CR0, 4YY

Except in the USA, this book is sold subject to the condition that it shall not, by way of trade or otherwise, be lent, resold, hired out, or otherwise circulated without the publisher's prior consent in any form of binding or cover other than that in which it is published and without a similar condition including this condition being imposed on the subsequent purchaser

Lazarus:

That Beautiful Blonde

LAMBBOOKS

Acknowledgements

The material in this book is adapted from 'The Poem of the Man+God' (The Gospel As Revealed To Me) by Maria Valtorta, first approved by Pope Pius XII in 1948, when, in a meeting on February 26th 1948, witnessed by three other priests, he ordered the three priest present to "Publish this work as it is".

In 1994, the Vatican heeded to the calls of Christians worldwide and have begun to examine the case for the Canonization of Maria Valtorta (Little John).

The Poem of the Man God was described by Pope Pius' confessor as "edifying". Mystical revelations have long been the province of priests and the religious. Now, they are accessible to all. May all who read this adaptation, also find it edifying. And through this light, may Faith be renewed.

Special Thanks to the Centro Editoriale Valtortiano in Italy for permission to quote from the Poem of the Man God by Maria Valtorta, nick named, Little John.

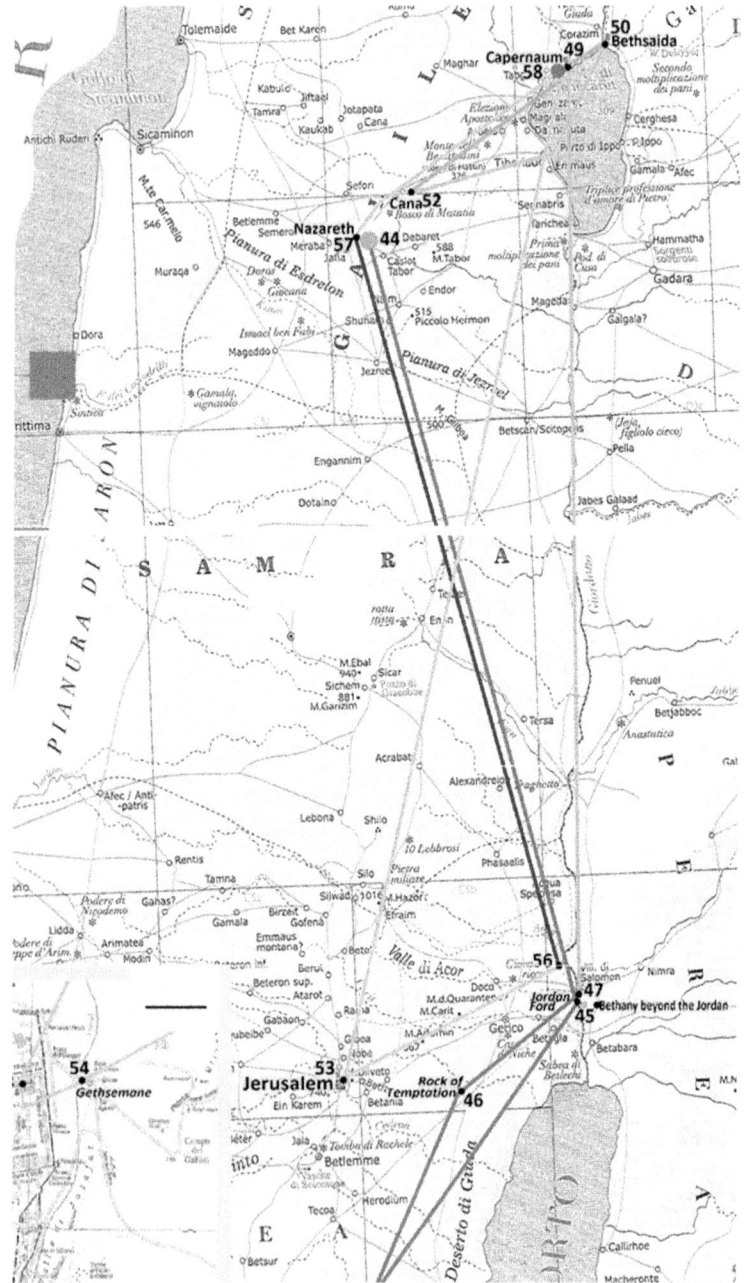

Contents

Jesus With Judas Iscariot Meets Simon Zealot And John   12

Jesus Cries On Account Of Judas And Simon Zealot Comforts Him   19

Jesus Meets Lazarus At Bethany   28

Jesus And Isaac Near Doco. Departure Towards Esdraelon 39

Return To Nazareth After Leaving Jonahs   46

The Next Day In The House In Nazareth   58

Jesus On The Lake Of Tiberias. Lesson To His Disciples Near The Same Town   67

Jesus In The Sea-Town Receives Letters Concerning Jonah 82

Jesus At Doras' House. Death Of Jonah   94

Jesus In The House Of Lazarus. Martha Speaks Of The Magdalene   115

Jesus With Judas Iscariot Meets Simon Zealot And John

'Are You sure he will come? ' Asks Judas Iscariot as he walks up and down with Jesus near one of the gates within the Temple enclosure.

'I am certain. He was leaving Bethany at dawn and at Gethsemane he was to meet My first disciple...'

There is a pause. Then Jesus stops in front of Judas and stares at him, studying him closely. Then He places a hand on Judas' shoulder and asks: 'Why, Judas, do you not tell Me your thoughts?'

'What thoughts? I have no special thought, Master, at the present moment. I ask You even too many questions. You certainly cannot complain of my muteness.'

'You ask Me many questions and You give Me many details on the town and its inhabitants. But you do not unburden yourself to Me. What do you think it matters to Me, what you tell Me about the wealth of people and the members of this or that family? I am not an idler who has come here to while away the time. You know why I have come. And you may well realize that I am concerned with being the Master of My disciples, as the most important thing. I therefore want sincerity and trust from them.

Was your father fond of you, Judas?'

'He was very fond of me. He was proud of me. When I went back home from school, and even later, when I went back to Kerioth from Jerusalem, he wanted me to tell him everything. He took an interest in everything I did and he would rejoice if they were good things, he would comfort me if they were not so good, if sometimes, You know, we all make mistakes – if I had made a mistake and had been blamed for it, he would show me the fairness of the reproach I had received, or the injustice of my action. But he did it so gently... he seemed an older brother. He always ended by saying: "I am saying this because I want my Judas to be just. I want to be blessed through my son." My father...'

Jesus, Who has carefully observed how moved Judas is at the recall of the memories of his father, says: 'Now, Judas, be sure of what I am going to tell you. Nothing will make your father so happy, as your being a faithful disciple. Your father, who brought you up as you said, must have been a just man and his soul will rejoice, where he is awaiting the light, seeing that you are My disciple. But in order to be such, you must say to yourself: "I have found my lost father, the father who was like an older brother to me, I have found him in my Jesus, and I will tell Him everything, as I used to tell my beloved father, over whose death I am still mourning, that I may receive from Him guidance, blessings or a kind reproach." May God grant it, and above all may you behave so that Jesus will always say to you: "You are good. I bless you."'

'Oh! Yes, Jesus! If You love me so much, I will strive to be good, as You want and my father wanted me to be.

And my mother will no longer have an aching pain in her heart. She used to say: "You have no guide now, my son, and you still need one so much." When she knows that I have You!'

'I will love you as no other man could possibly love you, I will love you so much, I do love you. Do not disappoint Me.'

'No, Master, I will not. I was full of conflicts. Envy, jealousy, eagerness to excel, sensuality, everything clashed in me against the voice of my conscience. Even quite recently, see? You caused me to suffer. That is: no, not You. It was my wicked nature... I thought I was Your first disciple... and, now You have just told me that You already have one.'

'You saw him yourself. Do you not remember that at Passover I was in the Temple with many Galileans?'

'I thought they were friends... I thought I was the first one to be chosen for such destiny, and that I was therefore the dearest.'

'There are no distinctions in My heart between the first and the last. If the first one should err and the last one were a holy man, then there would be a distinction in the eyes of God. But I will love just the same: I will love the holy living man with a blissful love, and the sinner with a suffering love. But here is John coming with Simon. John, My first disciple, Simon, the one of whom I spoke to you two days ago. You have already seen Simon and John. One was ill...'

'Ah! The leper! I remember. Is he already Your disciple?'

'Since the following day.'

'And why did I have to wait so long?'

'Judas?!'

'You are right. Forgive me.'

John sees the Master, points Him out to Simon and they make haste.

John and the Master kiss each other. Simon, instead, throws himself at Jesus' feet and kisses them, exclaiming: 'Glory to my Saviour! Bless Your servant that his actions may be holy in the eyes of God and that I may glorify Him and bless Him for giving You to me.'

Jesus places His hand on Simon's head: 'Yes, I bless you to thank you for your work. Get up, Simon. This is John, and this is Simon: here is My last disciple. He also wants to follow the Truth. He is therefore a brother to you all.'

They greet each other: the two Judaeans inquisitively, John heartily.

'Are you tired, Simon?' asks Jesus.

'No, Master. With my health I have recovered a vitality I never felt before.'

'And I know you make good use of it. I have spoken to many people and they all told Me that you have already instructed them about the Messiah.'

Simon smiles happily. 'Also last night I spoke of You to one who is an honest Israelite. I hope You will meet him one day. I would like to take You to him.'

'That is quite possible.'

Judas joins in the conversation: 'Master, You promised to come with me, in Judaea.'

'And I will. Simon will continue to teach the people on My coming. The time is short, My dear friends, and the people are so many. I will now go with Simon. You two will come and meet Me this evening on the road to the Mount of Olives and we will give money to the poor. Go now.'

When Jesus is alone with Simon, He asks him: 'Is that person in Bethany a true Israelite?'

'He is a true Israelite. His ideas are the prevailing ones, but he is really longing for the Messiah. And when I said to him: "He is now among us", he replied at once: "I am blessed because I am living this hour."'

'We shall go to him one day and take our blessing to his house. Have you seen the new disciple?'

'I have. He is young and seems intelligent.'

'Yes, he is. Since you are a Judaean, You will bear more with him than the others will, because of his ideas.'

'Is that a desire, or an order?'

'A kind order. You have suffered and You can be more indulgent. Sorrow teaches many things.'

'If You give me an order, I will be totally indulgent to him.'

'Yes. Be so. Perhaps Peter, and he may not be the only one, will be somewhat upset seeing how I take care and worry about this disciple. But one day, they will understand... The more one is deformed, the more assistance one needs.

The others... oh! The others form properly, also by themselves, by simple contact. I do not want to do

everything by Myself. I want the will of man and the help of other people to form a man. I ask you to help Me... and I am grateful for the help.'

'Master do You think he will disappoint You?'

'No. But he is young and was brought up in Jerusalem.'

'Oh! near You he will amend all the vices of that town... I am sure. I was already old and hardened by bitter hatred, and yet I have changed completely after seeing You...'

Jesus whispers: 'So be it!' Then in a loud voice: 'Let us go to the Temple. I will evangelize the people.'

Jesus Cries On Account Of Judas And Simon Zealot Comforts Him

Jesus is in very fertile country, full of magnificent orchards and vineyards with huge bunches of grapes beginning to turn gold or ruby. He has just finished speaking and is now sitting in an orchard, eating some fruit offered to Him by the farmer.

'It's a pleasure for me, Master, to quench Your thirst... .'says the farmer.'...Your disciple had spoken to us of Your wisdom but we were still astonished when we listened to You. Close as we are to the Holy City, we go there often to sell our fruit and vegetables, and then we go up to the Temple and listen to the rabbis. But they do not speak as You do. We used to come away saying: "If that is so, who will be saved?" With You, it is entirely different! Oh! We seem to be so light-hearted! Although adults, we feel like children in our hearts. I am a... rough man and I am not good at making myself understood. But I am sure You understand me!'

'Yes, I do. You mean that, although you have an adult's knowledge and maturity, after listening to the Word of God, you feel simplicity, faith and purity revive in your heart, as though you were a child again, without fault or malice, but with so much faith, as when you were taken to the Temple for the first time by your mother, or you prayed on her knees. That is what you mean.'

'Yes, that, just that. You are fortunate because you are always with Him' he says to John, Simon and Judas who are sitting on a low wall, eating juicy figs. 'And I am honoured because You were my guest for one night. I am not afraid of any misfortune in my house, because You have blessed it.'

Jesus replies: 'A blessing is efficacious and lasting if the souls of men are faithful to the Law of God and to My doctrine... answers Jesus.'... Otherwise its grace-giving ceases. And it is only fair. Because if it is true that God grants sunshine and fresh air to the good and to the bad; that they may live, and become better if they are good, and be converted if they are bad. It is also just that the Father's protection should turn elsewhere as a punishment for the wicked, to remind them of God, by means of some pain.'

'Is pain not always evil?'

'No, My friend. It is evil from a human point of view, but from a supernatural one it is good. It increases the merits of just people, who accept it without despairing or rebelling and they offer it, as they offer themselves with resignation, as a sacrifice to expiate their own imperfections and the faults of the world, and it is a redemption for those who are not good.'

'It is so difficult to suffer!' says the farmer, who has been joined by his relatives, about ten people in all, adults and children.

'I know that man finds it difficult. And knowing that he would find it so difficult, the Father had not given His children any sorrow. It came with sin. But how long does sorrow last on the earth? in the life of a man? A short time. It is always short, even if it lasts a whole lifetime. Now I say: is it not better to suffer for a short time rather than forever? Is it not better to suffer here than in Purgatory? Consider that time there is multiplied a thousand times to one. Oh! I solemnly tell you: you ought not to curse pain, but bless it, and you should call it "grace" and "mercy".'

'Oh! Your words, Master! They are as pleasant to us as honeyed water from a cool amphora to a man parched with summer thirst. Are You really going away tomorrow, Master?'

'Yes, I am going tomorrow. But I will come back again. To thank you for what you have done for Me and My friends, and to ask you for some more bread and a rest.'

'You will always find them here, Master.'

A man with a donkey laden with vegetables comes near.

'Here I am, If your friend wishes to go... My son is going to Jerusalem for the big Parasceve market.'

'Go, John. You know what you have to do. In four days' time we will meet again. My peace be with you.' Jesus embraces and kisses John and Simon does the same.

'Master' says Judas. 'If You will allow me, I would like to go with John. I am anxious to see a friend of mine. He goes to Jerusalem every Sabbath. I would go with John as far as Bethphage and then proceed on my own... He is a friend of our family... You know... my mother told me...'

'I have not asked you any question, My friend.'

'It breaks my heart having to leave You. But in four days'

time I will be with You again. And I will be so faithful that I will even bore You.'

'You may go. In four days' time, at dawn, be at the Fish Gate. Goodbye and may God watch over you.'

Judas kisses the Master and then goes near to the little donkey that has started to trot along the dusty road.

Evening falls and the country becomes silent. Jesus has not moved from where He was sitting when John and Judas departed. Simon watches the peasants irrigating their fields. Then Jesus gets up, goes round to the back of the house, and walks along the orchard. He wants to be alone. He goes as far as a thicket of huge pomegranate trees and low bushes that look like gooseberry bushes but have no berries on them. Jesus hides behind the thicket. He kneels down. He prays... and then He bows down with His face on the grass and He weeps. A disheartened crying; with deep interrupted sighs without sobs, but so sad.

Some time passes thus until twilight but not so dark as to prevent seeing. And in the faint light Simon's disfigured but honest face suddenly appears above a bush. He looks round as one searching for something and sees the crouched figure of the Master, completely covered by His dark blue mantle that blends in with the dark ground confusing him. Only His fair hair and His hands joined in prayer, and protruding above His head which is resting on His wrists, catches Simon's eye. Simon looks at Him with his large kind eyes and understands that Jesus is sad because of His sighing.

'Master,' calls Simon, with his thick almost purple lips.

Jesus looks up.

'You are crying, Master? Why? May I come near You?' Simon's expression is one of astonishment and sorrow. He is definitely not a handsome man and to add to his disfigured features and his dark olive complexion, he also bears the deep bluish scars from his disease. But his glance is so gentle that his ugliness disappears.

'Come, Simon, My friend.'

Jesus sits on the grass and Simon sits down beside Him.

'Why are You sad, Master? I am not John and I am not capable of giving You what John gives you. But I would like to give You every possible comfort, and I am only sorry that I am not able to do so. Tell me. Have I displeased You these last few days to the extent that it depresses You to stay with me?'

'No. My good friend. You have never displeased Me since the first moment I saw you. And I think you will never cause Me to shed tears.'

'Well, then, Master? I am not worthy of Your confidence. But, on account of my age, I could be Your father and You know how anxious I have always been to have children... Allow me to caress You as if You were my son and let me be a father and mother to You in this hour of pain. It is Your Mother that You are in need of to forget so many things...'

'Oh! Yes! It is My Mother!'

'Well, while waiting to have comfort in Her, grant Your servant the joy of consoling You. You are crying, Master, because someone has displeased You. For several days Your face has been like the sun darkened by clouds. I have been watching You. Your goodness hides the wound, that we may not hate him who wounds You.

But the wound is a painful and abhorrent one. But tell me, my Lord: why do You not remove the source of Your pain?'

'Because it would be useless from a human point of view and it would not be charitable.'

'Ah! You are aware that I am speaking of Judas! It is because of him that You are suffering. How can You, the Truth, tolerate that liar? He lies shamelessly. He is more deceitful than a fox and more closed than a rock. He has now gone away. What for? How many friends has he got? I am sorry to leave You. But I would like to follow him and see... Oh! My Jesus! That man... send him away, my Lord.'

'It is useless. What is to be, will be.'

'What do You mean?'

'Nothing special.'

'You allowed him to go with pleasure, because You were disgusted with his behaviour at Jericho.'

'It is true, Simon. I tell you once again: what is to be, will be. And Judas is part of this future. He is to be there, too.'

'But John told me that Simon Peter is very frank and full of ardour... Will he suffer Judas?'

'He must stand him. Also Peter is destined for a part, and Judas is the canvas on which he must weave his part, or, if you prefer, Judas is the school where Peter will learn more than with anyone else. Also idiots are capable of being good with John and understanding souls like John's. But it is difficult to be good with people like Judas, and to understand souls like Judas' and to be a doctor and a priest for them. Judas is your living teaching.'

'Ours?'

'Yes. Yours. The Master will not be on the earth forever. He will leave after eating the hardest bread and drinking the sourest wine. But you will stay to continue Me... and you must know. Because the world does not end with the Master. It will last longer, until the final return of Christ and the final judgement of man. And I solemnly tell you that for every John, Peter, Simon, James, Andrew, Philip, Bartholomew, Thomas, there are at least seven Judases. And many, many more!...'

Simon is thoughtful and silent. Then he says: 'The shepherds are good. Judas scorns them. But I love them.'

'I love them and praise them.'

'They are simple souls, such as You like.'

'Judas has lived in town.'

'His only excuse. But there are many people who have lived in towns, and yet... When will You come to my friend?'

'Tomorrow, Simon. And I will come with pleasure, because we are by our- selves, just you and I. I believe he is a learned and experienced man, like you.'

'And he suffers a lot... In his body and even more in his heart. Master... I would like to ask You a favour: if he does not speak to You of his grief, please do not ask him any question about his family.'

'I will not. I am on the side of those who suffer, but I do not force anybody's confidence. Tears deserve respect.'

'And I did not respect them... But I felt so sorry for You...'

'You are My friend and you have already given a name to My sorrow. I am an unknown Rabbi for your friend. When he knows Me... then... Let us go. It is dark. Do not let us keep our tired guests waiting. Tomorrow at dawn we will go to Bethany.'

Jesus Meets Lazarus At Bethany

It is early on a very clear summer morning and the sun, already above the horizon, is rising higher and higher, smiling at the charming earth; all the previous night's stars seem to have turned into gold and gem dust, now settled on all stems and leaves and sparkling with dew. Even the siliceous chips of the stones strewn on the ground and now wet with dew, seem like diamond powder or gold dust.
Jesus and Simon are now walking along a little side road that departs from the main road at a sharp 'V' angle, heading towards magnificent orchards and fields of flax as tall as a man and almost ready to be cut. Farther away, there are large bright red spots of poppies amongst other stubble in other fields.

'We are already in the property of my friend. You can see, Master, that the distance was within the prescription of the Law. I would never take the liberty of deceiving You. Behind that apple orchard there is the garden wall and the house. I made You come along this short cut to be within the prescribed mile.'
'Your friend is very wealthy!'
'Yes, very. But he is not happy. He owns property also

elsewhere.'
'Is he a Pharisee?'
'His father was not. He... is very observant. I told You: a true Israelite.'

They walk on. Ahead of them, there is a high wall and beyond it, trees and more trees, through which the house begins to emerge. A rise in the ground where they walk prevents them from seeing the garden that is as beautiful as a park.
They go round a corner and come up level with the wall that has branches of roses entwined and splendid sweet smelling jasmines in dewy corollas, hanging down from the top. Simon knocks with a heavy bronze knocker at the heavy wrought iron gate.

'It is too early to go in, Simon,' Jesus remarks.
'Oh! My friend gets up at sunrise as he finds comfort only in his garden or in books. Night is a torture for him. Please do not delay further to give him Your joy.'
A servant opens the gate.
'Good morning, Aseus. Tell your master that Simon Zealot has come with his Friend.'
The servant lets them in and says; 'Your servant greets you. Come in. Lazarus› house is open to his friends.' and then he runs away.
Simon, who is familiar with the place, turns away from the central avenue and instead follows a path that runs in the direction of a jasmine bower between rose hedges.

Lazarus emerges from the bower shortly afterwards, in a snow white linen garment and walking with difficulty as one suffering from leg trouble. He is tall, thin and pale

with short hair that is neither thick nor curly, and a little sparse beard confined to the lower part of his chin. When he sees Simon, he waves affectionately and then runs as best as he can towards Jesus and throws himself on his knees, bending down to the ground to kiss the hem of Jesus' tunic;

'I am not worthy of so much honour...' says Lazarus. 'But since Your holiness stoops to my misery, come, my Lord, come in and be the Master in my poor house.'
'Rise, My friend. And receive My peace.'
Lazarus gets up and kisses Jesus' hands and looks at Him with veneration not devoid of curiosity.
They walk towards the house.
'How anxiously I have waited for You, Master! Every morning, at dawn, I would say: "He will come today", and every evening I said: "I have not seen Him today, either."'
'Why were you expecting Me so anxiously?'
'Because... whom are we in Israel expecting, but You?'
'And do you believe that I am the Expected One?'
'Simon has never lied, neither is he a boy that gets excited over nothing. Age and sorrow have made him as mature as a wise man. In any case... even if he had not recognized Your true nature, Your deeds would have spoken and said that You are a "Saint" Who accomplishes the deeds of God, must be a man of God. And You accomplish them. And You do things in a way that says how truly You are the Man of God. My friend came to You because of the fame of Your miracles and he received a miracle. And I know that Your way is strewn with miracles. Why, then, not believe that You are the Expected One? Oh! It is so sweet to believe what is good! We have to feign to believe as good, many things that are not good, for the sake of peace because it would be

useless to change them; many dubious words that seem adulation, praise, kindness of heart and instead are sarcasm and blame, poison concealed by honey. We must pretend we believe them although we know they are poison, blame, sarcasm... we must do so because... it is not possible to do otherwise. And we are weak against a whole world that is strong. And we are alone against a whole world that is hostile to us... why, then, should we have difficulty in believing what is good? On the other hand the time is ripe and the signs of the time are here. What might still be missing to make belief certain and beyond all possible doubt, should be supplied by our anxiety to believe and to appease our hearts in the certainty that the expectation is finished and that the Redeemer has come, the Messiah is here... He Who will give peace to Israel and to the children of Israel, Who will let us die without anguish, knowing that we have been redeemed, and will enable us to live without that nostalgic feeling for our dead ones... Oh! the dead! Why mourn the death if not because, as they no longer have children, they have not yet the Father and God?'
'Has your father been dead long?'
'Three years, and my mother seven... but I no longer lament their deaths... I also would like to be where I hope they are awaiting Heaven.'
'In which case you would not have the Messiah as your guest.'
'That is true. Now I am in a better position than they are because I have You... and my heart calms down because of this joy. Come in, Master. Grant me the honour of making my house Yours. Today is the Sabbath and I cannot invite friends to honour You...'
'Neither do I wish that. Today I am all for Simon's friend

and Mine.'

They go into a beautiful hall, where some servants are ready to receive them. 'Please follow them' says Lazarus. 'You will be able to refresh yourselves before the morning meal.' And while Jesus and Simon go into another room, Lazarus gives instructions to the servants. The house displays wealth and refinement...

... Jesus drinks some milk, which Lazarus insists on serving personally, before sitting at the table for the morning meal.

'I have found the man who is willing to purchase your property and to pay the price that your agent fixed as a fair one. He will not deduct one drachma.' says Lazarus to Simon.

'But is he willing to comply with my conditions?'

'Yes, he is. He accepts everything, providing he gets the property. And I am happy because at least I know who my neighbour is. However, as you do not want to be present at the transaction, so he also wishes to remain unknown to you. And I would ask you to yield to his request.'

'I see no reason why I should not. You, my friend, will take my place... Whatever you do, is well done. It is enough for me that my faithful servant is not put out... Master, I am selling, and as far as I am concerned, I am happy that I have nothing more that may tie me to anything that is not Your service. But I have an old faithful servant, the only one left after my misfortune. And, as I have already told You, he has always helped me during my isolation, looking after my property, as if it were his own, nay, with the help of Lazarus, passing it off as his own, in order to save it and thus subsidize me. Now it would not be fair if I should leave him homeless, now that he is old. I have decided that a small house, near the boundary of the property, should be his and that part of the money should be given to him for his future maintenance. Old people, You know, are like ivy: having lived always in one place, they suffer too much being torn away from it. Lazarus wanted my servant with him, because he is good. But I preferred thus. The old man will not suffer so much...'

'You are good, too, Simon. If everybody were as just as you are, My mission would be easier...' remarks Jesus.

'Do You find the world averse, Master?' asks Lazarus.

'The world?... No. The strength of the world: Satan. If he were not the master of men's hearts and did not hold them in his possession, I would not find any resistance. But Evil is against Good, and I have to defeat evil in every man to put good into them... and they are not all willing...'

'It is true. They are not willing! Master: what words do You use to convert and convince those who are sinful? Words of severe reproach, like the ones that fill the history of Israel against guilty people, and the Precursor is the last to use them, or words of mercy?'

'I use love and mercy. Believe Me, Lazarus, a loving glance has more power on those who have fallen, than a curse.'

'And if love is mocked at?'

'One must insist again. Insist to the very utmost. Lazarus, do you know those lands where quick sands swallow unwary people?'

'Yes, I do. I have read about them because in my situation I read a lot, both out of enthusiasm and to pass the long sleepless hours at night. I know there are some in Syria and in Egypt and there are some near the Chaldeans. And I know that they are like suckers; They suck what they catch. A Roman says they are the mouths of Hell, where pagan monsters live. Is that true?'

'No, it is not true. They are only special formations of the earth. Olympus has nothing to do with them. People will stop believing in Olympus and still exist and the progress of mankind will only be able to give a more truthful explanation of the fact, but will not eliminate it. Now I say to you: since you read about them, you may also have read how a person who has fallen into them can be saved.'

'Yes. By means of a rope thrown to the person or by means of a pole or even a branch. Sometimes a small thing is sufficient to give a sinking man the minimum support to hold on to and in addition, the necessary calm, without struggling, to await rescue.'

'Well. A sinner, a man possessed, is one who has been swallowed by a deceitful soil, the surface of which is covered with flowers, whereas underneath it is quicksand. Do you think that if a man knew what it means to give Satan the possession of even an atom of himself, he would do it? But he does not know... and after... Either the astonishment and the poison of Evil paralyse him, or drive him mad and to avoid the remorse of being lost he struggles, he clings to other sands, he stirs up huge waves with his rash movements and thus hastens his own end. Love is the rope, the wire, the branch you mentioned. We must insist, insist... until it is caught. A word... forgiveness... a forgiveness greater than the fault... just to stop the sinking and await God's assistance. Lazarus, do you know the power of

forgiveness? It brings God to assist the rescuer... Do you read much?'
'Yes, I do. But I do not know whether I do the right thing. My disease and... and other things have deprived me of many of the delights of men... and now, I have but the passion for flowers and books... For plants and also for horses... I know that I am criticised for it. But how can I go to my estate in this condition (and he uncovers two huge legs all bandaged up) on foot or riding a mule? I must use a cart, and a fast one. That is why I bought some horses, of which I am now very fond, I admit. But if You tell me that that is wrong... I will have them sold.'
'No, Lazarus. These are not corrupting things. What upsets the soul and drives away from God is cause of corruption.'

'Now, Master. What I would like to know is this. I read a lot. I have but this comfort. I like to learn... I think that after all it is better to know than to do wrong, it is better to read than to do other things. But I do not read only our pages. I like to learn about the world of other peoples and I am attracted by Rome and Athens. Now, I am aware of the great evil that befell Israel when she became corrupted by the Assyrians and the Egyptians and of the great harm done to us by Hellenistic governments. I do not know whether a man can do himself the same harm that Judas did himself and us, his children. What is Your opinion on the matter? I am anxious to be taught by You, as You are not a rabbi, but the wise and divine Word.'
Jesus stares at him for a few seconds, His glance penetrating and distant at the same time. He seems to pierce Lazarus' opaque body and scrutinise his heart and penetrating even further, He appears to see... 'Are you upset by what you read? Jesus asks at last. 'Does it

detach you from God and His Law?'
'No, Master. On the contrary, it urges me to make comparisons between our true God and pagan falseness. I make comparisons and I meditate on the glories of Israel, her just people, the Patriarchs, the Prophets and the questionable figures of other peoples' histories. I compare our philosophy, if we can call so the Wisdom that speaks in our sacred texts, with the poor Greek and Roman philosophies which contain sparks of fire but not the blaze that bums and shines in the books of our Wise Men. And after, with greater veneration, I bow down with my soul to adore our God Who speaks in Israel through deeds, people and our books.'
'Well, then, continue to read... It will help you to understand the pagan world... Continue. You may continue. There is no ferment of evil or of spiritual gangrene in you. You, therefore, may read without any fear. The love you have for your God makes sterile the profane germ that reading might spread in you. In all man's actions there is the possibility of good and of evil. It depends on how they are accomplished. Love is not a sin, if one loves in a holy way. Work is not a sin, if one works when it is the right time. To earn is not a sin, if one is satisfied with what is honest. To educate oneself is not a sin, providing the
education does not kill the idea of God in us. Whereas it is a sin to serve also at the altar, if one does it for one's own benefit. Are you convinced, Lazarus?'
'Yes, Master. I asked other people the same question and they scorned me... But You give me light and peace. Oh! If everybody heard You! Come, Master. Amongst the jasmines there is a cool breeze and silence. It is sweet to rest under their cool shade awaiting the evening.'

Lazarus

And they go out.

Jesus And Isaac Near Doco. Departure Towards Esdraelon

'And I tell You, Master, that humble people are better...' Isaac reports to Jesus. '...the ones I spoke to either laughed at me or ignored me. Oh! The little ones at Juttah! '
They are seated in a group on the grass by the riverbank and Judas interrupts Isaac, exceptionally calling the shepherd by name;
'Isaac, I am of your opinion. We waste our time and lose our faith dealing with them. I am giving it up.'
'I will not but it makes me suffer. I will give up only if the Master tells me. For years I have been accustomed to suffering out of loyalty to the truth. I could not tell lies to get into the good graces of the mighty ones. And do you know how many times they came to make fun of me in the room where I was ill, promising help – oh! they were certainly false promises – if I would say that I had lied and that You, Jesus, were not the New-Born Saviour?! But I could not lie. If I had lied I would have denied my own joy, I would have killed my only hope, I would have rejected You, my Lord! Reject You! In my dark misery in my dreary illness there was always a sky strewn with stars above me: the face of my mother who was the only joy of my orphan life, the face of a bride who was never

mine and whom I continued to love even after her death. These were the two minor stars. And the two major stars, like two most pure moons: Joseph and Mary smiling at the New-Born Baby and at us poor shepherds, and Your bright, innocent, kind, holy, holy, holy face, in the centre of the sky of my heart. I could not reject that sky of mine! I did not want to deprive myself of its light as there is no other so pure. I would have rather rejected my own life or I would have lived in torture rather than reject You, My blessed remembrance, my New-Born Jesus! '
Jesus lays His hand on Isaac's shoulder and smiles.
'So you insist?' persists Judas
'I do. Today, tomorrow and the day after again. Someone will come.'
'How long will the work last? '
'I don't know. But believe me. It is enough not to look either ahead or behind and do things day by day. And in the evening, if we have worked with profit, we say: "Thank You, my God". If without profit, just say: "I hope in Your help for tomorrow." '
'You are wise.'
'I don't even know what it means. But I do in my mission what I did during my sickness. Thirty years of infirmity is no trifling matter! '
'Ehi! I believe that. I was not yet born and you were already an invalid.'
'I was ill. But I never counted those years. I never said: "Now it is the month of Nisan again, but I am not blossoming again with the roses. Now it is Tishri and I still languish here." I went on speaking of Him both to myself and to good people. I realised that the years were passing because the little ones of bygone days came to bring me their wedding confections or the cakes for the

birth of their little ones. Now, if I look back, now that from old I have become young, what do I see of my past? Nothing. It is past.'

'Nothing here. But in Heaven it is "everything" for you, Isaac, and that "everything" is waiting for you' says Jesus. And then speaking to everyone: 'You must do so. I do so Myself. We must go on. Without getting tired. Tiredness is one of the roots of human pride. And so is haste. Why is man annoyed by defeats? Why is he upset by delays? Because pride says: "Why say 'no' to me? So much delay for me? This is a lack of respect for the apostle of God." No, My friends. Look at the whole universe and think of Him Who made it. Meditate on the progress of man and consider his origin. Think of this hour which is now being completed and count how many centuries have preceded it. The universe is the work of a calm creation. The Father did not do things in a disorderly way; He made the universe in successive phases. Man is the work of patient progress, the present man, and he will progress more and more in knowledge and in power. And such knowledge and power will be holy or not holy, according to his will. But man did not become skilled all at once. The First Parents, expelled from the Garden, had to learn everything, slowly, progressively. They had to learn the simplest things: that a grain of corn is tastier if ground into flour, then kneaded and then baked. And they had to learn how to grind it and bake it. They had to learn how to light a fire. How to make a garment by observing the fleece of animals. How to make a den by watching beasts. How to build a pallet by watching nests. They learned how to cure themselves with herbs and water by observing animals that do so by instinct. They learned to travel across deserts and seas, studying the stars, breaking in horses, learning how to balance boats on water by watching the shell of a nut floating on the water of a stream. And how many failures before success! But man succeeded. And he will go farther. But he will not be happier on account of his progress because he will become more skilled in evil than in good. But he will make progress. Is Redemption not a patient work? It was decided centuries and centuries ago. It is happening now after being prepared for centuries. Everything is patience. Why be impatient then? Could God not have made everything in a flash? Was it not possible for man, gifted with reason, created by the hands of God, to know everything in a flash? Could I not have come at the beginning of centuries? Everything was possible. But nothing must be violence. Nothing. Violence is always against order and God, and what comes from God is order. Do not attempt to be superior to God.'

'But, then, when will You be known? '

'By whom, Judas? '

'By the world! '

'Never! '

'Never? But are You not the Saviour? '

'I am. But the world does not want to be saved. Only one in a thousand will be willing to know Me and only one in ten thousand will really follow Me. And I will say even more; I will not be known even by My most intimate friends.'

'But if they are Your intimate friends, they will know You.'

'Yes, Judas. They will know Me as Jesus, as Jesus the Israelite. But they will not know Me as He Who I am....' and with resigned discouragement, Jesus opens

His hands and holding the, out turned outwards, He continues, with sorrow written on His face, looking at neither man nor Heaven but only at His future destiny of a betrayed person '...I solemnly tell you that I will not be known by all My intimate friends. To know means to love with loyalty and virtue... and there will be who does not know Me.'
'Do not say that' implores John.
'We follow You, to know You more and more' says Simon, and the shepherds in chorus.
'We follow You as we would follow a bride and You are dearer to us than she could be; we are more jealous of You than of a woman....' Says Judas '...Oh! no. We know You already so much that we cannot ignore You any longer.' and pointing at Isaac, Judas continues 'He says that to deny Your remembrance of a New-Born Baby would have been more distressing than losing his life. And You were but a new-born baby. We know You as Man and Master. We listen to You and see Your works. Your contact, Your breath, Your kiss: they are our continuous consecration and our continuous purification. Only a satan could deny You after being Your close companion.'
'It is true, Judas. But there will be one.'
'Woe to him! I will be his executioner.'
'No. Leave justice to the Father. Be his redeemer. The redeemer of this soul that is inclined towards Satan. But let us say goodbye to Isaac. It is evening. I bless you, My faithful servant. You now know that Lazarus of Bethany is our friend and is willing to help My friends. I am going. You are staying here. Prepare the parched land of Judaea for Me. I will come later. In case of need you know where to find Me. My peace be with you' and Jesus blesses and

kisses His disciple.

Return To Nazareth After Leaving Jonahs

It is time to say goodbye and Jesus and His disciples are standing at the door of a poor hut, with Jonah and other poor peasants, lit by a light so faint, it seems to be blinking.

'Will I not see You again, my Lord?' asks Jonah. 'You have brought light to our hearts. Your kindness has turned these days into a feast that will last all our lives. But You have seen how we are treated. A mule is taken better care of than we are. And trees receive more human attention; they are money. We are only millstones that earn money and we are used until we die of excessive toil. But Your words have been as many loving caresses. Our bread seemed more plentiful and it tasted better because You shared it with us; this bread which he does not even give to his dogs. Come back to share it with us, my Lord. Only because it is You, I dare say that. It would be an insult to offer anyone else shelter and food which even a beggar would disdain. But You...'
'But I find in them a heavenly perfume and flavour because in them there is faith and love. I will come, Jonah. I will come back. You stay in your place, tied like an animal to the shafts. May your place be Jacob's

ladder. And in fact angels go and come from Heaven down to you, carefully gathering all your merits and taking them up to God. But I will come to you. To relieve your spirit. Be faithful to Me, all of you. Oh! I would like to give you also human peace. But I cannot. I must say to you: go on suffering. And that is very sad for One Who loves...'

'Lord, if You love us, we no longer suffer. Before we had no one to love us...Oh! If I could, at least, see Your Mother! '

'Do not worry. I will bring Her to you. When the weather is milder, I will come with Her. Do not risk incurring cruel punishments on account of your anxiety to see Her. You must wait for Her as you wait for the rising of a star, of the evening star. She will appear to you all of a sudden, exactly as the evening star, which is not there one moment, and a moment later it shines in the sky. And you must consider that even now She is lavishing Her gifts of love on you. Goodbye, everybody. May My peace protect you from the harshness of him who torments you. Goodbye, Jonah. Do not cry. You have waited for so many years with patient faith. I now promise you a very short wait. Do not weep; I will not leave you alone. Your kindness wiped My tears when I was a New-Born Baby. Is Mine not sufficient to wipe yours?'

'Yes... but You are going away... and I have to remain here...'

'Jonah, My friend, do not make Me go away depressed because I cannot comfort you ...'

'I am not crying, my Lord... But how will I be able to live without seeing You, now that I know that You are alive?'

Jesus caresses the forlorn old man once again and then

goes away. But standing on the edge of the miserable threshing floor, Jesus stretches His arms out and blesses the country. Then He departs.

'What have You done, Master?' asks Simon who has noticed the unusual gesture. .

'I put a seal on everything. That no demon may damage things and thus cause trouble to those wretched people. I could do no more…'

'Master, let us walk on a little faster. I would like to tell You something which I do not want the others to hear.' They move farther away from the group and Simon begins to speak: 'I wanted to tell You that Lazarus has instructions to use my money to assist all those who apply to him in Jesus' name. Could we not free Jonah? That man is worn out and his only joy is to be with You. Let us give him that. What is his work worth here? If instead he were free, he would be Your disciple in this beautiful yet desolate plain. The richest people in Israel own fertile estates here and they exploit them with cruel extortion, exacting a hundredfold profit from their workers. I have known that for years. You will not be able to stop here long, because the sect of the Pharisees rules over the country and I do not think it will ever be friendly to You. These oppressed and hopeless workers are the most unhappy people in Israel. Your heard it Yourself, not even at Passover have they peace, neither can they pray, whilst their severe masters, with solemn gestures and affected exhibitions, take up prominent positions in front of all the people. At least they will have the joy of knowing that You exist and of listening to Your words repeated to them by one who will not alter one single letter. If You agree Master, please say so, and Lazarus will do what is necessary.'

That Beautifull Blonde

'Simon, I knew why you gave all your property away. The thoughts of men are known to Me. And I loved you also because of that. By making Jonah happy, you make Jesus happy. Oh! How it torments Me to see good people suffer! My situation of a poor man despised by the world afflicts Me only because of that. If Judas heard Me, he would say: "But are You not the Word of God? Give the order and these stones will become gold and bread for the poor people." He would repeat Satan's snare. I am anxious to satisfy people's hunger. But not the way Judas would like. You are not yet sufficiently mature to grasp the depth of what I want to say. But I will tell you: if God saw to everything He would rob His friends. He would deprive them of the chance of being merciful and fulfilling the commandment of love. My friends must possess this mark of God in common with Him: the holy mercy consisting in deeds and words. And the unhappiness of other people gives My friends the opportunity to practice it.
Have you understood what I mean?'
'Your thought is a deep one. I will ponder Your words. And I humble myself as I see how dull-minded I am and how great God is Who wants us to be gifted with all His most sweet attributes so that He may call us His children. God is revealed to me in His manifold perfections by every ray of light with which You illuminate my heart. Day by day, like one advancing in an unknown place, the knowledge of the immense Thing which is the Perfection Which wants to call us His "children" progresses in me and I seem to climb like an eagle or to dive like a fish into two endless depths like sky and sea, and I climb higher and higher and dive deeper and deeper but I never touch the end. But what

is, therefore, God?'
'God is the unattainable Perfection, God is the perfect Beauty, God is the infinite Power, God is the incomprehensible Essence, God is the unsurpassable Bounty, God is the indestructible Mercy, God is the immeasurable Wisdom, God is the Love that became God. He is the Love! He is the Love! You say that the more you know God in His perfection, the higher you seem to climb and the deeper to dive into two endless depths of shadeless blue... But when you understand what is the Love that became God, you will no longer climb or dive into the blue but into a blazing vortex and you will be drawn towards a beatitude that will be death and life for you. You will possess God, with a perfect possession, when, by your will, you succeed in understanding and deserving Him. You will then be fixed in His perfection.'
'O Lord...' exhales Simon, overwhelmed.
They walk in silence until they reach the road where Jesus stops to wait for the others.
When they regroup again, Levi kneels down: 'I should be leaving, Master. But Your servant asks You a favour. Take me to Your Mother. This man is an orphan like me. Do not deny me what You give him, that I may see the face of a mother...'
'Come. What is asked in My Mother's name, I grant in My Mother's name.'

The sun, although about to set, blazes down unto the grey- green dome of the thick olive trees laden with small well- shaped fruit but only penetrates the tangle of branches enough to provide a few tiny eyelets of light whereas the main road, on the other hand, embedded between two banks, is a dusty blazing dazzling ribbon.

Alone and walking fast among the olive trees, Jesus smiles to Himself...He smiles even more happily when He reaches a cliff....Nazareth....its panorama flickering in the heat of the blazing sun...and Jesus begins to descend and quickens His step.
Now on the silent, deserted road, He has protected His head with His mantle and, no longer minding the sun, is walking so fast that the mantle is blowing at His sides and behind Him so that He seems to be flying.

Now and again, the voice of a child or of a woman from inside a house or a kitchen garden reaches Jesus where He is walking in the shady spots provided by garden trees whose branches extend into the road. He turns into a half shaded road where there are women gathered around a cool well and they all salute Him, welcoming Him in shrill voices.

'Peace to you all... But please be silent. I want to give My Mother a surprise.'
'Her sister-in-law has just gone away with a pitcher of cool water. But she is coming back. They are left without any water. The spring is either dry or the water is absorbed by the parched land before reaching Your garden. We don't know. That's what Mary of Alphaeus was saying. There she is... she is coming.'
Not having seen Jesus yet, the mother of Judas and James, with an amphora on her head and another in her hand, is shouting; 'I'll be quicker this way. Mary is very sad, because Her flowers are dying of thirst. They are the ones planted by Joseph and Jesus and it breaks Her

heart to see them withering.'
'But now that She sees Me...' says Jesus appearing from behind the group of women.
'Oh! My Jesus! Blessed You are! I'll go and tell...'
'No. I will go. Give Me the amphoras.'
'The door is half shut. Mary is in the garden. Oh! How happy She will be! She was speaking of You also this morning. But why come in this heat! You are all perspiration! Are You alone?'
'No. With friends. But I came ahead of them to see My Mother first. And Judas?'
'He is at Capernaum. He often goes there.' says Mary. And she smiles as she dries Jesus' wet face with her veil. The pitchers now ready, Jesus takes two, tying one at each end of His belt which He throws across His shoulder and then takes a third one in His hand. Then He walks away, turns round a corner, reaches the house, pushes the door, enters the little room that seems dark in comparison with the bright sunshine outside. Slowly, He lifts the curtain at the garden door and He watches. Mary is standing near a rose-bush with Her back to the house, pitying the parched plant. Jesus lays the pitcher on the floor and the copper tinkles against a stone. 'Are you here already, Mary?' says His Mother without turning round.
'Come, come, look at this rose! And these poor lilies. They will all die if we do not assist them. Bring also some small canes to hold up this falling stalk.'
'I will bring You everything, Mother.'

Mary springs round and for a moment, She remains with Her eyes wide open then with a cry She runs with outstretched arms towards Her Son, Who has already opened His arms and is waiting for Her with the most loving smile.

'Oh! My Son!'

'Mother! Dear!'

Their embrace is a long and loving one and Mary is so happy that She does not feel how hot Jesus is. But then She notices it: 'Why, Son, did You come at this time of the day? You are purple red and perspiring like a sodden sponge. Come inside. That I may dry and refresh You. I will bring You a fresh tunic and clean sandals. My Son! My Son! Why go about in this heat! The plants are dying because of the heat and You, My Flower, are going about.'

'It was to come to You as soon as possible, Mother.'

'Oh! My dear! Are You thirsty? You must be. I will now prepare...'

'Yes, I am thirsty for Your kisses, Mother. And for Your caresses. Let Me stay like this, with My head on Your shoulder, as when I was a little boy... Oh! Mother! How I miss You!'

'Tell Me to come, Son, and I will. What did You lack because of My absence? The food You like? Clean clothes? A well-made bed? Oh! My Joy, tell Me what You lacked. Your servant, My Lord, will endeavour to provide.'

'Nothing, but You...'

Hand in hand, Mother and Son go into the house. Jesus sits on the chest near the wall, embraces Mary Who is in front of Him, resting His head on Her heart and kissing Her now and again. Now He stares at Her: 'Let Me look at You to My heart's content, holy Mother of Mine.'

'Your tunic first. It is not good for You to remain so damp. Come.' Jesus obeys. When He comes back wearing a fresh looking tunic, they resume their sweet

conversation.
'I have come with My disciples and friends but I left them in Melcha's wood. They will come tomorrow at dawn. I... I could not wait any longer. My Mother!...' and He kisses Her hands. ' Mary of Alphaeus has gone away to leave us alone. She also understood how anxious I was to be with You. Tomorrow...tomorrow You will attend to My friends and I to the Nazarenes. But this evening You are My Friend and I am Yours. I brought You... Oh! Mother: I found the shepherds of Bethlehem. And I brought You two of them: they are orphans and You are the Mother of all men. And more so of orphans. And I brought You also one who needs You to control himself. And another one who is a just man and has suffered so much. And then John... And I brought You the recollections of Elias, Isaac, Tobias, now called Matthew, John and Simeon. Jonah is the most unhappy of them all. I will take You to him... I promised him. I will continue to look for the others. Samuel and Joseph are resting in the peace of God.'
'Were You at Bethlehem?'
'Yes, Mother. I took there the disciples who were with Me. And I brought You these little flowers, that were growing near the stones of the threshold.'
'Oh!' Mary takes the withered stems and kisses them.
'And what about Anne?'
'She died in Herod's slaughter.'
'Oh! Poor woman! She was so fond of You!'
'The Bethlehemites suffered a lot. But they have not been fair to the shepherds. But they suffered a lot...'
'But they were good to You then!'
'Yes. And that is why they are to be pitied. Satan is jealous of their past kindness and urges them to evil

things. I was also at Hebron. The shepherds, persecuted...'
'Oh! To that extent?!'
'Yes, they were helped by Zacharias, who got them jobs and food, even if their masters were hard people. But they are just souls and they turned their persecutions and wounds into merits of true holiness. I gathered them together. I cured Isaac... and I gave My name to a little boy... At Juttah, where Isaac was languishing and where he came back to life again, there is now an innocent group, called Mary, Joseph and Jesai...'
'Oh! Your Name!'
'And Yours and the name of the Just One. And at Kerioth, the fatherland of a disciple, a faithful Israelite died resting on My heart. Out of joy, having found Me... And then... Ah! how many things I have to tell You, My perfect Friend, sweet Mother! But first of all, I beg You, I ask You to have so much mercy on those who will be coming tomorrow. Listen: they love Me... but they are not perfect. You, Teacher of virtue... oh! Mother, help Me to make them good... I would like to save them all...' Jesus has slipped at Mary's feet. She now appears in Her Motherly majesty.
'My Son! What do You want Your poor Mother to do better than You do?'
'To sanctify them... Your virtue sanctifies. I brought them here deliberately, Mother... one day I will say to You: "Come", because it will then be urgent to sanctify souls, that I may find them willing to be redeemed. And I will not be able by Myself... Your silence will be as eloquent as My words. Your purity will assist My power. Your presence will keep Satan away... and Your Son, Mother, will feel stronger knowing that You are near Him. You will

come, will you not, My sweet Mother?'
'Jesus! Dear Son! I have a feeling that You are not happy... What is the matter, Creature of My heart? Was the world hostile to You? No? It is a relief to believe it... but... Oh! Yes. I will come. Wherever You wish, as and when You wish. Even now, in this blazing sunshine, or by night, in cold or wet weather. You want Me? Here I am.'
'No. Not now. But one day... How sweet is our home. And Your caresses! Let Me sleep thus, with My head on Your knees. I am so tired! I am still Your little Son...' And Jesus really falls asleep, tired and exhausted, sitting on the mat, His head on the lap of His Mother, Who happily caresses His hair.

The Next Day In The House In Nazareth

At daybreak the next day, Mary, in Her light blue dress, barefooted, light and noiseless as a butterfly, moves actively about the house, touching wall and other things. Then, carefully, She opens the front door without making a sound, looks at the deserted road and then leaves the door half open.

She tidies up, opens doors and windows, goes into the workshop-since abandoned by the Carpenter and where She now keeps Her looms-and also bustles about in there; carefully, She covers one of the looms still fed with the beginnings of newly woven cloth and smiles at Her thoughts whilst as She looks at it.

Out in the garden, the doves gather on Her shoulders and with short flights from one shoulder to the other, quarrelsome and jealous for Her love, they accompany Her to the food storage closet where She finds some grain for them.' Here, stay here today. Don't make any noise. He is so tired!'
Then She takes some flour into the anteroom by the stone oven and begins to make bread, kneading it and smiling delightfully. How Mother smiles to-day. Once

again, She is the young Mother of the Nativity, made young again by Her joy.

She separates a lump of dough and setting it aside, covers it and then resumes Her work, getting warmer whilst Her hair grows lighter in colour as it becomes slightly powdered with flour.

Quietly, Mary of Alphaeus comes.' Are You working already?'
'Yes, I am baking bread, and look: the honey cakes He likes so much.'
'You make the cakes. The dough is quite bulky. I'll work it for You.'
Mary of Alphaeus, a more robust country woman, works at the bread with enthusiasm, whilst Mary mixes butter and honey to the cakes. She makes many round shaped ones and places them on a metal plate.
'I do not know how to inform Judas... James does not dare... and the others... '
Mary of Alphaeus sighs.
'Simon Peter is coming today. He always comes with the fish on the second day after the Sabbath. We will send him to Judas.'
'If he is willing to go...'
'Oh! Simon never says no to Me.'
'May peace be on this day of yours' says Jesus emerging. The two women start, hearing His voice.
'Are You already up? Why? I wanted You to sleep...'
'I slept like a child in its cradle, Mother. I am afraid You have not slept...'
'I watched You sleeping... I always did so when You were a baby. You always smiled in Your sleep and that smile of Yours remained all day long in My heart like a pearl...

But last night, Son, You were not smiling. You kept sighing as one who is afflicted...' Mary, sore at heart, looks at Him.

'I was tired, Mother. The world is not like this house, where everything is honesty and love. You... You know Who I am and can thus understand what it is for Me to be in touch with the world. It is like walking along a foul muddy road. Even if a man is careful, he will get splashed with mud and the stench will penetrate him even if he endeavours not to breathe... and if he is a man who loves cleanliness and pure air, You can imagine how troublesome it is...'

'Yes, Son, I understand. But it grieves Me that You should suffer...'

'Now I am with You and I do not suffer. There is only the memory... But it serves to increase the joy of being with You.' And Jesus bends down to kiss His Mother.

He caresses also the other Mary, who has just come in all flushed, after lighting the oven fire.

'We will have to inform Judas.' It is the worry of Mary of Alphaeus.

'It is not necessary. Judas will be here, today.'

'How do You know?' Jesus smiles and is silent.

'Son, every week, this day, Simon Peter comes. He comes to bring the fish caught early in the night. And he arrives here shortly after daybreak. He will be happy today. Simon is good. He always helps us whilst he is here. Does he not, Mary?'

'Simon Peter is honest and good' says Jesus.' But also the other Simon whom You will see shortly, is a kind-hearted man. I am going to meet them. They must be about to arrive.'

And Jesus goes out whilst the women put the bread into

the oven and then go into the house, where Mary puts on Her sandals and then comes back wearing a snow-white linen dress.
Some time goes by and whilst they wait, Mary of Alphaeus says:' You did not have time to finish that work.'
'It will soon be finished. And My Jesus will have the relief of shade without having His head burdened.'
The door is pushed from outside.' Mother: here are My friends. Come in.'
The disciples and shepherds go in all together. Jesus is holding by their shoulders the two shepherds and He leads them towards His Mother:' Here are two sons looking for a mother. Be their joy, Woman.'
'You are welcome... You?... Levi... You? I do not know, but according to your age, as He told Me, you must be Joseph. That name is sweet and sacred in this house. Come, come. It is with joy that I say to you: My house welcomes you and a Mother embraces you, in remembrance of the love you in your father had for My Child.'
The shepherds seem spellbound, so enraptured are they.
'Yes, I am Mary. You saw the happy Mother. I am still the same. Also now I am happy seeing My Son among faithful hearts.'
'And this is Simon, Mother.'
'You deserved the grace because you are good. I know. And may the grace of God be always with you.'
Simon, who is more experienced in the customs of the world, bows down to the ground, his arms crossed over his chest, and says:' I salute You, true Mother of Grace and now that I have met both the Light and You, Who are more gentle than the moon, I will not ask the Eternal

Father for anything else.'
'And this is Judas of Kerioth.'
'I have a mother but my love for her fades away, compared to the veneration I feel for You.'
'No, not for Me. For Him. I am, only because He is. I want nothing for Myself.
I only ask for Him. I know how you honoured My Son in your town. But I say to
you: let your heart be the place where He receives the highest honour from you. Then I will bless you with a motherly heart.'
'My heart is under the heel of your Son. A happy oppression. Only death will undo my loyalty.'
'And this is our John, Mother.'
'I have not been worried ever since I knew you were with My Jesus. I know you and My mind is at peace when I know that you are with My Son. I bless you, My peace.' She kisses him.
Peter's harsh voice is heard from outside:' Here is poor Simon bringing his greetings and...' He has come in and is dumbfounded. Then he throws on to the floor the round basket that was hanging from his shoulder and he throws himself on his knees saying:' Ah! Eternal Lord! But... No, You should not have done that to me, Master! You were here... and did not let poor Simon know! May God bless You, Master! How happy I am! I could not bear to be without You any longer!' And he caresses Jesus' hand without listening to Him Who keeps repeating:' Get up, Simon. Will you get up?'
'Yes, I will get up. But... Hey, you, boy! ...' Peter says to John '....at least you could have come to tell me! Now run quick. Go to Capernaum and tell the others... and Judas' household first of all. Your son is about to arrive,

woman....Be quick. Just imagine you are a hare being chased by dogs.'
John leaves laughing.
Peter, now up at last, is still holding Jesus' thin hand in his short thickset ones marked with swollen veins and he kisses it without letting it go, although he also appears to be anxious to hand over the fish that is in the basket on the floor.' Eh! no. I don't want You to go away again without me. Never again, never again such a long time without seeing You! I will follow You like a shadow follows a body and the rope follows the anchor. Where have You been, Master? I kept wondering: "Oh! Where will He be? What will He be doing? And will that boy, John, be able to look after Him? Will he make sure that Jesus does not get too tired? That He is not left without food?" Eh! I know You... You have lost weight! Yes, You have. He did not take proper care of You! I will tell him that... But where have You been, Master? You are not telling me anything!'
'I am waiting for you to give Me a chance to say one word!'
'It's true. But... Ah! To see You is like having a new wine. It goes to your head just with its smell. Oh! My Jesus.'
Peter is almost in tears with Joy.
'I also missed you. I missed you all, although I was with dear friends. Here, Peter. These two men have loved Me since I was a New-Born Baby. Even more! They have suffered because of Me. Here is a son who lost his father and mother on account of Me. But now he has so many brothers in you all, has he not?'
'Of course, Master. If by chance, the Devil should love You, I would love him because he loves You. I see that you are poor, too. So we are equal. Come here that I may

kiss you. I am a fisherman but my heart is more tender than a dove's. And it is sincere. Don't pay attention if I am rough. I am hard outside. Inside I am all butter and honey. But with good people... because with evil ones...'
'And this is the new disciple.'
'I think I have already met him...'
'Yes, he is Judas of Kerioth and Your Jesus was made welcome in that town because of him. I ask you to love each other, even if you are from different regions. You are all brothers in the Lord.'
'And I will treat him as such, if he will be such. Eh! Yes... (Peter stares at Judas, a frank warning glance), yes, I may as well say so, so you will understand me at once and properly. I will tell you: I do not think much of Judaeans in general and of the citizens of Jerusalem in particular. But I am honest. And upon my honesty I can assure you that I will put aside all the ideas I have of you and that I want to see in you only a brother disciple. It is up to you now not to make me change my mind and my decision.'
'Have you such preconceived ideas, Simon, also with regard to me?' asks the Zealot smiling.
'Oh! I had not seen you. With regard to you? Oh! no. Honesty is painted on your face. Goodness comes from your heart, like sweet smelling oil from a porous vase. And you are an elderly man, which is not always a merit. Sometimes, the older one gets, the more false and worse one becomes. But you are one of those who behave like vintage wines. The older they get, the better and purer they become.'
'You have judged correctly, Peter' says Jesus.' Now come. While the women are working for us, let us stop under the cool bower. How lovely it is to be with friends! We will

then go, all together, through Galilee and farther. Well, not all. Now that Levi is satisfied, he will go back to Elias to tell him that Mary sends him Her greetings. Is that all right, Mother?'

'That I bless him, as well as Isaac and the others. My Son has promised to take Me along with Him... and I will come to you, the first friends of My Child.'
'Master, I would like Levi to take to Lazarus the letter You know about.'

'Have it ready, Simon. Today is a full feast day. Levi will go away tomorrow evening. In time to be there before the Sabbath. Come, My friends...'
And they go into the green kitchen garden.

Jesus On The Lake Of Tiberias. Lesson To His Disciples Near The Same Town

Jesus along with His thirteen disciples, are in two boats on lake Galilee; Jesus is with Peter in Peter's boat, together with Andrew, Simon, Joseph and Jesus' two cousins; Judas Thaddeus and James.
The two sons of Zebedee-John and James-are in the second boat along with Judas Iscariot, Philip, Thomas, Nathanael and Matthew.
The two boats, not being used for fishing but for passage only, are sailing fast before a cool north wind that lightly ripples the water leaving a fine lace-work of foam on the turquoise blue of the beautiful clear lake.
The two boats sail in company-with Peter's boat only a few yards ahead of the second boat- leaving two wakes that meet almost immediately to form a pleasant bright sparkling froth.
Being only a few yards apart, the disciples trade remarks and comments; the Galileans illustrate and explain the various spots of the lake to the Judaens, their trades, the important people who live in the area, the distance from Capernaum where they started to the place of arrival in Tiberias.

Sitting at the prow, Jesus enjoys the beauties of the

nature around Him; the quiet, the blue sky and the blue lake with its circular border of green shores where many white villages stand out against the green of the countryside.

Almost lying on a bundle of sails at the very front of the prow, He pays no attention to the conversation of the disciples. Often, He lowers His head to look at the sapphire mirror of the lake as though to study its depth and the creatures living in the clear water.
Twice, Peter addresses Him to enquire whether He is bothered by the sun, already risen from the east and now shining full on to the boat and warm though not hot. The second time, Peter also asks if Jesus wants some bread and cheese like the others. But Jesus wants neither tent nor bread and Peter leaves Him alone.

A few small leisure boats- the size of a shallop- fitted with purple canopies and soft cushions, cut across the course of the fishermen's boats accompanied by shouts, bursts of laughter and the smell of perfumes. The leisure boats are full of beautiful women, merry Romans, some Palestinians and a few Greeks. A slender young man, brown as an almost ripe olive and smartly dressed in a short red tunic with heavy Greek fret borders and held tight at the waist by a belt that is a masterpiece of a goldsmith, says:
'Hellas is beautiful! But not even my Olympic fatherland has this blue and these flowers. It is really not surprising that the goddesses left it to come here. Let us spread flowers, roses and our compliments to the goddesses, no longer Greek but Judaean...'And he spreads on the women in his boat, petals of magnificent roses, and

throws some into a nearby boat.
A Roman replies: 'Spread them, spread them, Greek! But Venus is with me. I do not spread roses, I pick them from this beautiful mouth. It is sweeter!' And bending down, he kisses the open smiling lips of Mary of Magdala, who is leaning on cushions with her blond head in the lap of the Roman.

The little boats are now in front of the two big ones and because of the inexperience of the rowers as well as the sudden gusts of wind, the boats nearly collide.

'Be careful, if your lives are dear to you' shouts Peter, who veers wildly and shifts the helm to avert a collision. Insults from the men and shouts of fear from the women go from boat to boat.
'Get out of the way, you dirty Jewish dogs' the Romans insult the Galileans.

Peter and the other Galileans do not let the insults pass. Peter, flushing like a cockerel, stands on the edge of the boat that is pitching wildly and with his hands on his hips, gives tit for tat not sparing Romans, Greeks, Jews or Jewesses. He assails the women with such courteous titles that cannot be repeated and the squabble lasts until the tangle of keels and oars is loosed and they all go their separate ways.

Whilst all this is happening, Jesus does not move from His place and remains sitting, His mind far away, without a glance or a word to the boats or the passengers.
Leaning on one elbow, He looks at the far away shore, as if nothing was happening. A woman throws a flower at Him and laughs but He does not stir. The flower almost

hits His face, then falls onto the boards and ends up under the feet of the furious Peter
As the boats are about to move away, the Magdalene stands up and following the indication of one of her partners in vice, turns her beautiful eyes towards the serene face of Jesus, Whose mind is still so far away. How far away from this world that face is!...

'Say, Simon!' asks Judas Iscariot. 'Since you are a Judaean like me, tell me. That beautiful blonde in the Roman's lap, the one who stood up a few minutes ago, isn't she the sister of Lazarus of Bethany?'
'I don't know' is the sharp reply of Simon the Cananean. 'I came back amongst the living only a short while ago and she is a young woman... '
'You are not going to tell me that you do not know Lazarus of Bethany, I hope! I know very well that you are his friend and that you have been there also with the Master.'
'And if it were so?'
'And since it is so, I say that you must know also the sinner who is Lazarus' sister. Even the dead know her! People have been talking about her for the last ten years. She began to be light-headed as soon as she reached puberty. But for over four years! You must be aware of the scandal, even if you were in the "valley of the dead". The whole of Jerusalem talked about her. And Lazarus shut himself up at Bethany... He did the right thing, after all. No one would have set foot in his magnificent house in Zion, where she also came and went. I mean: no holy living person. In the country... well!... In any case she is always around, but never at home... She is certainly at Magdala now... With a new lover... Are you not answering

me? Can you give me the lie?'
'I am not giving you the lie. I am silent.'
'So it is she! You have recognized her, too!'
'I saw her when she was a child and she was pure then. I have seen her again now... But I recognize her. Although lewd, she is the living image of her mother, a holy woman.'
'Well, then, why were you on the point of denying that she is your friend's sister?'
'We always endeavour to conceal our sores and those of the people we love. Particularly when one is honest.'
Judas gives a forced laugh.
'You are quite right, Simon. And you are honest' remarks Peter.
'And did you recognize her? You certainly go to Magdala to sell your fish and I wonder how many times you have seen her!...'
'My boy, you must know that when your back is broken after an honest day's work, you are not interested in women. You only love the honest bed of your wife.'
'Eh! Everybody likes beautiful things! At least, if for no other reason than to look at them.'
'Why? To say: "It is no food for my table"? No, certainly not. I have learned many things from the lake and from my job and this is one of them: a fish of fresh and calm water is not fit for salt water or a vorticose water course.'
'What do you mean?'
'I mean that everybody should keep his place to avoid dying an evil death.'
'Did the Magdalene make you feel as if you were dying?'
'No, I am tough. But tell me: are you not feeling well, perhaps?'
'Me? Oh! I didn't even look at her!...'

'You liar! I am sure that you were consumed with envy because you were not on this boat, to be closer to her... you would have put up even with me to be nearer... So much so, that you honour me with your conversation because of her, after so many days of silence.'
'Me? She would not have even seen me! She was always looking at the Master!'
'Ah! Ah! Ah! And he says that he was not looking at her! How could you see where she was looking if you did not look at her?'
They all laugh at Peter's remark, except Judas, Jesus and Simon Zealot.

'Is that Tiberias?' Jesus asks Peter, putting an end to the discussion, which He feigns He has not heard.
'Yes, Master, it is. I will now haul.'
'Wait. Can you stop in that small quiet bay? I would like to speak to you only.'
'I will measure the depth and let You know.' And Peter lowers a long pole into the water and moves slowly towards the shore. 'Yes, I can, Master. Shall I go closer to the shore? '
'As far as you can. There is shade and solitude. I like it.'
Peter steers towards the shore and when the boat is about fifteen yards away from shore he says' I would now touch.'
'Stop. And you come as close as possible and listen.'
Jesus leaves His place and sits in the middle of the boat, on a plank placed crosswise. The disciples in His boat sit round Him whilst the other boat is in front of Him.

'Listen. You may think that I do not pay attention to your conversation and consequently, that I am a lazy teacher who does not look after his pupils. You must know that My soul does not leave you one moment. Have you ever seen a doctor who studies a patient affected by a disease not yet identified and presenting contrasting symptoms? He keeps an eye on him. After he visits him, he watches him both when he sleeps and is awake, in the morning and in the evening, when he speaks and when he is silent because every symptom may help to identify the hidden disease and suggest a cure. I do the same with you. I hold you by means of invisible but most sensitive threads, that are grafted into Me and they transmit to Me even the lightest vibrations of your ego. I allow you to believe that you are free, that you may reveal yourselves for what you are, which happens when a schoolboy or a maniac thinks he is not being watched by his overseer. You are a group of people, but you form a nucleus, that is, one thing only. You are therefore a unit, which is formed as a body and which is to be studied in its individual features, which are more or less good, in order to shape it, amalgamate it, round it off, increase it in its polyhydric sides and make it a perfect unit. That is why I study you. And I study you also when you are sleeping. What are you? What are you to become? You are the salt of the earth. That is what you must become: the salt of the earth. With salt, meat and many other victuals are preserved from putrefaction. But if the salt were not salty, could it be used to salt? I want to salt the world with you, to have it seasoned with a celestial flavour. But how can you salt if you become tasteless?

What causes you to lose a celestial flavour? That which is human. Sea water, that is: the water of the real sea, is so salty that it is not good to drink, is it? And yet, if one takes a cup of sea water and pours it into an amphora of

fresh water, then one can drink it, because the sea water is so diluted that it has lost its biting strength. Mankind is like fresh water mixed to your celestial saltiness.
Again, suppose we could take a little stream of water from the sea and get it to flow into this lake, would you be able to trace that tiny stream? No. It would have been lost in the fresh water. That is what happens to you when you immerse, or rather, you submerge your mission in so much humanity.
You are men. I know. And who am I? I am He Who has all possible strength. And what do I do? I communicate such strength to you after calling you. But what is the use of communicating it to you, if you dissipate it under avalanches of human influences and sentiments?
You are, you must be the light of the world. I chose you: I, the Light of God amongst men, that you may continue to illuminate the world, after I have gone back to the Father. But can you illuminate if you are smoky lamps which have gone out? No. Nay, with your smoke – an ambiguous smoke is worse than a completely extinguished wick – you would darken the dim light that the hearts of men may still have.
Oh! Miserable are those who will apply to the apostles seeking God and instead of light will receive smoke! It will be scandal and death for them. But the unworthy apostle will be cursed and punished. Your destiny is a great one! And a great tremendous commitment as well! But remember that who has been given more, is obliged to give more. And you have been given the most, both in the way of education and of gifts. You are educated by Me, the Word of God, and you receive from God the gift of being "the disciples", that is, the continuators of the Son of God.

I would like you to meditate upon your election, to examine yourselves thoroughly, to weigh yourselves... and if anyone feels that he is suitable only to be a believer – I will not even say: if anyone feels he is but an unrepentant sinner; I only say: if anyone feels that he is suitable only to be a believer – but does not feel the strength of an apostle, let him withdraw.

The world is large, beautiful, sufficient, varied enough for those who love it! It offers all the flowers and all the fruit suitable for the stomach and the senses. I offer but one thing: holiness. And on the earth it is the meanest, the poorest, the roughest, the thorniest and the most persecuted thing that exists. In Heaven its meanness is changed into immensity, its poverty into riches, its thorniness into a flowery carpet, its hardness into a smooth pleasant path, its persecution into peace and beatitude. But here it is a hero's Labour to be a saint. That is all I can offer.

Are you willing to remain with Me? Do you not feel like staying? Oh! Do not be amazed or sorry. You will hear Me ask you this question many times. And when you hear it, please think that My heart weeps asking it, because it is wounded by your insensibility to your vocation. So examine your own consciences, then judge with honesty and sincerity, and then make up your minds. Make up your minds, so that you may not become reprobates. Say "Master, friends, I realize that I am not made for this life. I kiss you goodbye and I say to you: pray for me."

Better so than to betray. Better so... What do you say? Betray whom? Whom? Me. My cause, which is the cause of God because I am one thing with the Father. And yourselves, yes, you would betray yourselves, you would betray your souls, giving them away to Satan. Do you wish to remain Jews? I will not force you to change. But do not betray. Do not betray your souls, Christ and God. I swear that neither I, nor those faithful to Me will criticise you. Neither will they have you despised by the faithful crowd. A short while ago one of your brothers said a great word: "We always endeavour to conceal our sores and those of the people we love." And he who would go away, would be a sore, a cancer, which after growing in our apostolic body, would come off because of its total gangrene, leaving a painful mark, which we would carefully keep hidden.

No, do not cry, you who are the better ones. Do not cry. I bear you no grudge, neither am I intolerant seeing you so slow. You have just been chosen and I cannot expect you to be perfect. I will not even demand it after some years, after repeating one hundred or two hundred times the same things in vain. Nay, listen: in a few years' time you will be less fervent than now that you are novices.

Such is life... such is mankind... You lose impetus after the first leap. But (Jesus springs to His feet) I swear to you that I will win. Purified by natural selection, fortified by a supernatural mixture, you, better ones, will become My heroes. The heroes of Christ. The heroes of Heaven. The power of the Caesars will be like dust as compared to the regality of your priesthood. You, poor fishermen of Galilee, you, unknown Judaeans, you, mere numbers in the mass of present men, will become more famous, more acclaimed, more venerated than Caesar, and then all the Caesars the world ever had or will have. You will be known and blessed in the near future and in the most remote centuries until the end of the world. I appoint you to such sublime destiny because you are honestly willing. And I will outline the essential features of the apostolic

character, so that you may be fit for your destiny.
Be always vigilant and ready. Your loins should be always girded up and your lamps always lit as if you were to leave any moment or to run to meet someone who is arriving. You are in fact and will be until your death, the indefatigable pilgrims looking for wanderers; and until death puts them out, your lamps are to be held high up and lit to show the way to misguided souls coming towards the fold of Christ.

You are to be faithful to the Master Who appointed you to such service. That servant will be rewarded whom the master always finds vigilant and upon whom death comes in the state of grace. You cannot and must not say: "I am young, I have time for this and for that, and then I will think about my Master, my death, my soul! Young people die like old ones, and strong men like weak ones. And old and young, strong and weak are equally subject to the assaults of temptation. Be careful because the soul can die before the body and you may unknowingly carry around a putrid soul. The dying of a soul is so imperceptible! Like the death of a flower. Not a cry, not a convulsion... it inclines its flame like a tired corolla and goes out. Later, sometimes after a long time, sometimes immediately after, the body realizes it is carrying a verminous corpse within itself, it becomes mad with fear and commits suicide to avoid such union... Oh! it does not avoid it! It falls on to a swarm of snakes in Gehenna with its very verminous soul. Do not be dishonest like brokers or underhand dealers, who side with two opposite customers. Do not be false like politicians, who call this man and that man a "friend" whereas they are enemies to both of them. Do not act in

two different ways. You cannot laugh at God or deceive
Him. Behave with men as you do with God because an
insult to man is an insult to God. Let God see you as you
wish to be seen by men.

Be humble. You cannot reproach your Master for not
being so. I set the example. Do as I do. Be humble,
gentle, patient. That is how the world is conquered. Not
by violence or force. Be strong and violent against your
vices. Eradicate them at the cost of breaking your hearts.
Some days ago I told you to watch over your eyes. But
you do not know how to do it. I tell you: it would be
better to become blind by pulling out greedy eyes rather
than become lustful.

Be sincere. I am the Truth: both in sublime and human
things. I want you to be genuine, too. Why be deceitful
with Me, or your brothers, or your neighbour? Why cheat
people? Proud as you are, why do you not say: "I do not
want people to find out that I am a liar"? And be sincere
with God. Do you think you can deceive Him with long
manifest prayers? Oh! poor children! God sees into your
hearts!

Be chaste in doing good. Also in giving alms. An excise
man knew how to be so before his conversion. And are
you not capable? Yes, I am praising you, Matthew, for
your chaste weekly offer, which only the Father and I
knew was yours and I am quoting you as an example.
Also that is a form of chastity, My friends. Do not disclose
your goodness as you would not undress a young
daughter before a crowd of people. Be virgins in doing
good. A good act is virgin when it is free from any

connection with thoughts of pride and praise, or from incentives of pride.

Be faithful to your vocation to God, you cannot serve two masters; A nuptial bed cannot hold two brides at the same time. God and Satan cannot share your embraces. Man cannot, neither can God nor Satan, share a treble embrace conflicting with the three embracing one another. Be averse to the lust for gold as well as to the lust for the flesh, to the lust for the flesh as to the lust for power. That is what Satan offers you. Oh! his deceitful riches! Honour, success, power, wealth: obscene markets where your souls are the legal tender. Be satisfied with little. God gives you what is necessary. It is enough. He guarantees that for you as He does for the birds of the air and you are worth much more than birds. But He wants reliance and moderation from you. If you rely on Him, He will not disappoint you. If you are moderate, His daily gift will be sufficient for you.

Do not be pagans by being of God only by name. Those are pagans who love gold and power in order to appear as demigods more than they love God. Be holy and you will be like God in eternity. Do not be intolerant. Since you are all sinners, behave to others as you would like others to behave to you: that is, with mercy and forgiveness.

Do not judge. Oh! do not judge! You have only been with Me for a short time and yet you have seen how many times I, although innocent, have been wrongly judged and accused of non-existent sins. A bad judgement is an insult. And only true saints do not pay back in the offender's coin. Refrain therefore from offending so that you may not be offended. Thus you will not fail in your duties either to charity or to holy, dear, kind humility, which is Satan's enemy, together with chastity. Forgive, always forgive. Say: "I forgive, Father, that I may be forgiven by You of my numberless sins."

Improve hourly, with patience, perseverance, heroism. Who told you that it is not painful to become good? Nay, I tell you: it is the greatest labour. But the reward is Heaven and it is therefore worthwhile getting exhausted in such labour.

And love. Oh! What words shall I use to persuade you to love? None is suitable to convert you to love, poor men, instigated by Satan! So I say: "Father, hasten the hour of purification. This land and this flock of Yours are dry and diseased. But there is a dew that can cleanse and soothe them. Open its fountain. Open Me, Father. Here I am burning with the desire to fulfil Your will, which is also Mine and of the Eternal Love. Father, Father, Father! Look at Your Lamb and be Its Sacrificer." '

Truly inspired and standing with His arms stretched in the shape of a cross and His face raised towards the sky, Jesus, in His linen tunic and with the blue lake behind Him, seems a praying archangel.

Jesus In The Sea-Town Receives Letters Concerning Jonah

It is a beautiful sea-town with a wide, natural and well-protected gulf, that has a capacity for taking many ships. At the harbour, made even safer by the massive harbour wall, are ancient Roman war galleys with soldiers on board. The soldiers are disembarking either to relieve troops or to reinforce the garrison.

Jesus and His disciples are sitting at ease with the residents, in a humble house of a fisherman near the harbour, probably friends of Peter and John. Joseph is absent. And so is Judas Iscariot.
Speaking informally to the members of the family and other people who have come to listen to Him, Jesus' words are full of advice and comfort, such as only He can give.

Enters Andrew, returning from an errand with some loaves in his hands. Shy as he is, he blushes as he draws near, tortured by the attention he must be drawing to himself and rather than speak, he whispers:
'Master, could You come with me? There... there is some good to be done. But only You can do it.'
Without asking what good it is, Jesus gets up.

'Where are you taking Him?' asks Peter. 'He is so tired. It is supper time. They can wait for Him till tomorrow.'
'No... it must be done at once. It is...'
'Why don't you speak, you frightened gazelle? How can a great big strapping man be like that!... You look like a little fish caught in the net! '
Andrew's blushes deepen and Jesus defends him, drawing him to Himself. 'I like him thus. Leave him alone. Your brother is like wholesome water. It works noiselessly in the depths, it comes out from the earth like a very fine stream but it cures those who go near it. Let us go, Andrew.'
'I'm coming, too! I want to see where he takes You 'insists Peter.
'No, Master. Only You and I, alone.' implores Andrew. 'If there is a crowd it is impossible. It's a matter of love...'
'What's that? Are you playing the paranymph now?'
Ignoring his brother, Andrew says to Jesus: 'A man wants to repudiate his wife and... and I have spoken. But I am not capable. But if You speak... oh! You will succeed because the man is not a bad person. He is... he is... he will tell You.'
Without further ado, Jesus goes out with Andrew. Peter is momentarily undecided and then he then says: 'I will go. At least I want to see where they go.' And he goes out, although the others tell him not to.

As Andrew emerges from a narrow thronged street, Peter follows him onto and around a little square full of old women. Andrew threads his way through an arch that opens on to a wide yard surrounded by poor low little houses, still with Peter in tow.
Jesus goes into one of the little houses with Andrew

Lazarus

and Peter lies in wait outside. A woman sees him and asks: 'Are you a relative of Aava? And those two? Have you come to take her away?'
'Be quiet, you cackle of a hen! I am not to be seen.' answers Peter, casting withering glances at the woman who goes off to chat with other old women. But Peter is immediately surrounded by a circle of women, boys and men, who simply by commanding one another to be silent, make so much noise that give away their presence. Peter is consumed with anger...but to no avail.

The full, calm beautiful voice of Jesus floats out from inside the house, together with the broken voice of a woman and the hoarse voice of a man:
'If she has always been a good wife, why repudiate her? Have you ever wronged him?'
'No, Master, I swear it! I have loved him like the pupil of my eye' moans the woman.
And the man, sharp and hard: 'No. She never wronged me except in being sterile...' come the man's voice, hard and sharp. ' ..And I want children. I don't want God's malediction on my name.'
'It is not your wife's fault if she is such.'
'He lays the blame on me. On me and my relatives, as if we betrayed... '
'Woman, be sincere. Did you know that you were sterile?'
'No. I was and I am like all women. Also the doctor said so. But I am not successful in having children.'
'You can see that she has not betrayed you. She suffers for that too. Will you answer sincerely also: if she were a mother, would you repudiate her?'
'No. I swear it. There is no reason. But the rabbi said so and also the scribe: "A barren woman is the curse of

God on a house and it is your right and duty to give her a divorce libel and not to vex your virility by depriving yourself of children." I am doing what the Law states.'

'No. Listen. The Law says: "Do not commit adultery" and you are about to commit it. That is the original commandment and nothing else. And if on account of the hardness of your hearts Moses granted divorce, it was to prevent intrigues and concubinages hateful to God. Then your vice expanded more and more Moses' clause, creating the wicked chains and murderous stones which are the present lot of women, always victims of your arrogance, of your whims, of your deafness and your blindness to affections. I tell you: it is not legal to do what you want to do. Your action is an offence to God. Did Abraham perhaps repudiate Sarah? And Jacob, Rachel? And Elkanah, Anna? And Manoah, his wife? Do you know the Baptizer? You do? Well: was his mother not sterile up to her old age and then gave birth to the holy man of God, as Manoah's wife gave birth to Samson, and Anna of Elkanah to Samuel, and Rachel to Joseph, and Sarah to Isaac? To the husband's continence, to his compassion for his sterile wife, to his fidelity to marriage, God grants a prize, and a prize celebrated through centuries, as He grants consolation to the weeping sterile women, no longer sterile nor depressed, but glorious in the exultation of being mothers. You are not allowed to offend her love. Be just and honest. God will reward you beyond your merit.'

'Master, You are the only one to speak so... I did not know. I asked the doctors and they said to me: "Do it." But not one word to tell me that God rewards a good deed with gifts. We are in their hands... and they close our eyes and our hearts with an iron hand. I am not a

bad man, Master. Don't be angry with me.'
'I am not angry. I feel sorry for you more than I do for this weeping woman. Because her pain will end with her life. Yours will begin then, to last forever. Think about it.'
'No, it will not begin. I don't want it to begin. Will You swear to me by the God of Abraham that what You say is the truth?'
'I am the Truth and Wisdom. Who believes in Me will have justice, wisdom, love and peace.'
'I want to believe You. Yes, I want to believe You. I feel there is something in You which is not in the others. Well. I will now go to the priest and I will say to him: "I am not going to repudiate her any longer. I will keep her and I will only ask God to help me to feel less the pain of being childless." Aava: do not cry. We will ask the Master to come again to keep me good, and you... continue to love me.'

The woman cries louder because of the contrast between her previous sorrow and her present joy.
Jesus smiles. 'Do not cry. Look at Me. Look up woman.'
She looks up. She looks at His bright face through her tears.
'Come here, man. Kneel down beside your wife. I will now bless you and sanctify your union. Listen:..'
And in a thundering voice, with His hands stretched out over their bowed heads, Jesus prays:
' "Lord God of our fathers, Who made Adam with the dust of the soil and gave him Eve as a helpmate, that they might populate the earth with men, bringing them up in Your holy fear, descend with Your blessing and Your mercy, open and fecundate the womb that the Enemy had closed to lead them to a double sin of adultery and

despair. Have mercy on these two children, Holy Father, Supreme Creator. Make them happy and holy. May she be as prolific as a vineyard and he her protector, as the elm-tree supports the vine. Descend, o Life, to give life. Descend, o Fire, to inflame. Descend, o Power, to activate. Descend! Grant them that for the praise feast for the fruitful crops next year they may offer You their living sheaf, their first born, a son, sacred to You, Eternal Father, Who bless those who hope in You." '
The people no longer refrain themselves but gather together, with Peter in front of them all.
'Stand up. Have faith and be holy.'
'Oh! Stay, Master!' beg the reconciled couple.
'I cannot. I will come back. I will be here very often.'
'Stay, stay. Speak also to us!' shout the crowd. Jesus blesses but does not stop. He promises only to come back soon. And He goes to His hospitable house, followed by a small crowd.
'Inquisitive man: what should I do to you?' He asks Peter on the way.
'Whatever You wish. However, I was there...'
They enter the house and dismiss the crowd who are commenting on the words they've heard, and they sit down to supper.

But Peter's curiosity is not yet satisfied .'Master, will there really be a son? '
'Have you ever seen Me promise things which do not come true? Do you think that I would take the liberty of using the confidence in the Father to lie and deceive? '
'No... but... Could You do that to all married couples? '
'I could. But I do it only where I see that a son can be an incentive to holiness. I do not do it where it would be a

hindrance.'

Peter ruffles his grizzled hair and becomes quiet.

The shepherd Joseph comes in covered in dust like one who has walked a long way.

'You? Why are you here?' asks Jesus after a greeting kiss. 'I have some letters for You. Your Mother gave me them and one is from Her. Here they are.' And Joseph hands Him three small rolls of thin parchment, tied with a little ribbon. The largest one is sealed, the second one has only a knot and the third one shows a broken seal.' This one is from Your Mother' says Joseph, pointing at the one with the knot. Jesus unfolds it and reads it first in a low voice and then loud. "'To My beloved Son, peace and blessings. A messenger from Bethany arrived here at the first hour on the calends of the month of Elul. It was the shepherd Isaac, to whom I gave the kiss of peace and refreshments in Your name and out of gratitude on my part. He brought Me these two letters which I am sending on to You and he told Me that Your friend Lazarus of Bethany presses You to consent to his request.

My beloved Jesus, blessed Son and Lord, I also have two things to ask You. One is to remind You that You promised Me to call Your poor Mother to instruct Her in the Word. The other is that You should not come to Nazareth without speaking to Me first"'

Jesus stops all of a sudden, stands up, and goes towards James and Judas. He embraces them tightly and then repeats by heart the words: "'Alphaeus has returned to the bosom of Abraham at the last full moon and great was the mourning of the town...' The two sons weep on Jesus' chest, Who goes on: "'At the last hour he wanted You. But You were far away. But it is a consolation for

Mary, who considers it a sign of God's forgiveness and it must give peace also to My nephews." Have you heard? She says so. And She knows what She is saying.'
'Give me the letter' implores James.
'No, it would hurt you.'
'Why? What can it say that is more painful than the death of a father?...'
'That he cursed us' sighs Judas.
'No. Not so' says Jesus.
'You say so... not to pierce us. But it is so.'
'Read, then.'
And Judas reads: '"Jesus: I beg You, and also Mary begs You; do not come to Nazareth until the mourning is over. Their love for Alphaeus makes the Nazarenes unfair towards You and Your Mother cries because of that. Our good friend Alphaeus comforts Me and calms the town. The report by Aser and Ishmael on Chuza's wife caused a great stir. But Nazareth is now a sea agitated by different winds. I bless You, My Son, and I ask Your peace and blessing for My soul. Peace to My nephews. Mother".'
The apostles make their comments and comfort the weeping brothers. But Peter says: 'Are You not reading those? '
Jesus nods assent and opens Lazarus' letter. He calls Simon Zealot and they read together in a comer. Then they open the last roll and read it as well, discuss between themselves and the Zealot endeavours unsuccessfully to persuade Jesus about something. With the rolls in His hand, Jesus comes to the centre of the room and says: 'Listen, friends. We are one family and there are no secrets among us. And if it is compassion to conceal evil, it is justice to make good known. Listen to what Lazarus of Bethany writes: "To

Lord Jesus peace and blessing, and peace and health to my friend Simon. I received Your letter and, servant as I am, I placed my heart, my speech and all my means at Your service to make You happy and to have the honour of not being a useless servant. I went to Doras, to his castle in Judaea, to ask him to sell me his servant Jonah, as You wish. I confess that if I had not been requested by Simon, a faithful friend, on Your behalf, I would not have faced that mocking, cruel, impious jackal. But for You, my Master and Friend, I feel I can face also Mammon. Because I think that who works for You, is near You and consequently is protected. And I have certainly been helped, because, contrary to expectations, I won. The discussion was a hard one and his first refusals humiliating. Three times I had to bow down to that powerful slave- driver. He then forced me to wait some days. At last here is the letter. It befits the asp he is. And I almost dare not say to You: – Give in to gain Your ends –, because he is not worthy to have You. But there is no other way. I accepted on Your behalf and I signed. If I did the wrong thing, rebuke me. But believe me: I tried to serve You as well as I could. Yesterday a Judaean disciple of Yours came, stating that he came in Your name to find out whether there was any news to be taken to You. He said he was Judas of Kerioth. But I preferred to wait for Isaac to send the letter. And I was surprised that You had sent someone else since You know that Isaac comes here every Sabbath to rest. I have nothing else to tell You. Only, kissing Your holy feet, I beg You to bring them to Your servant and friend Lazarus, as promised by You. Health to Simon. To You, Master and Friend, a kiss of peace and a prayer for blessing. Lazarus".

And now the other one: "Health to Lazarus. I decided. You will have Jonah for twice the amount. But I make the following terms and I will not change them for any reason. I want Jonah to finish the harvests of the year, that is, he will be handed over at the moon of Tishri, at the end of the moon. I want Jesus of Nazareth to come personally to take him, and I will ask Him to enter my house, that I may meet Him. I want payment immediately after signing the contract.
Goodbye. Doras".'
'What a pest!' shouts Peter. 'But who is paying? I wonder how much he wants and we... we are always without a farthing!'
'Simon is paying. To make Me and poor Jonah happy. He is buying only the wreck of a man, who will not serve him at all. But he gains great merit in Heaven.'
'You? Oh!' They are all surprised. Even Alphaeus' sons forget their sorrow because of their amazement.
'It is he. It is just that it should be known.'
'It would also be just if it were known why Judas Iscariot went to Lazarus. Who sent him? Did You?'
But Jesus, very grave and pensive, does not reply to Peter. He comes out of His meditation only to say: 'Give some refreshment to Joseph and then let us go and rest. I will prepare a reply for Lazarus... Is Isaac still at Nazareth?'
'He is waiting for me.'
'We shall all go.'
'No. Your Mother says...'They are all in utter confusion.
'Be quiet. That is what I want. My Mother speaks with Her loving heart. I judge with My reason. I prefer to do it while Judas is away. And I want to hold out a friendly hand to My cousins, Simon and Joseph, and mourn

with them before the mourning is over. We will then go back to Capernaum, to Gennesaret, that is to the lake, awaiting the end of the month of Tishri. And we will take the Marries with us. Your mother needs affection. We will give it to her. And Mine needs peace. I am Her peace.'
'Do You think that at Nazareth... ?' asks Peter.
'I do not think anything. '
'Oh! Well! Because if they should hurt Her or cause Her sorrow!... They will have to deal with me!' says Peter completely upset.
Jesus caresses him but He is sad and lost in thought. Then He goes between Judas and James and sits down embracing them to comfort them. The others speak in low voices in order not to disturb their sorrow.

Jesus At Doras' House. Death Of Jonah

It is a cloudy late November day following one of the first rains of the dreary winter months in the plain of Esdraelon. Rain from the previous night has left the earth damp but not muddy. There's a damp wind saturated with moisture, that blows away the yellow leaves and pierces to the bone.

A few yokes of oxen ploughing the fields laboriously turn the rich heavy soil of the fertile plain, preparing it for seed. In some fields, there are men working as oxen, pushing the ploughshare with all the strength of their arms and chests, pressing their feet into the soil already turned, toiling like slaves in this work that is very hard also for robust bulls.

Jesus looks and notices and His face turns so sad as to weep. The shepherds are no longer here and Judas is still absent but the eleven disciples speak among themselves:
' Also a boat is small, poor and laborious...' says Peter. 'But it is one hundred times better than this pack-animal job!. Are they perhaps Doras' servants?' He asks.
'I don't think so: his fields are beyond that orchard, I think. And we can't see them yet.' replies Simon Zealot.

But Peter, always curious, leaves the road and walks along a hedge between two fields where four thin peasants, wet with perspiration and panting with fatigue, have sat down for a moment on its borders.

'Are you Doras' men?' Peter asks them.

'No, but we belong to his relative, to Johanan. And who are you?'

'I am Simon of Jonas, a fisherman of Galilee until the moon of Civ. Now I am Peter of Jesus of Nazareth, the Messiah of the Gospel.' Peter says with the respect and glory with which one would say: 'I belong to the high divine Caesar of Rome' and much more, too and his honest face is shines with joy in professing himself of Jesus.

'Oh! the Messiah! Where, where is He?' ask the four unhappy men.

'That one over there. The tall fair-headed one, clad in dark red. The one who is now looking here and is smiling waiting for me.'

'Oh!... If we went there... would He send us away?'

'Send you away? Why? He is the friend of the unhappy, the poor, the oppressed and I think that you... yes, you are just them...'

'Oh! we are indeed! But not like Doras' men. At least we have as much bread as we want and we are not lashed unless we stop working, but... '

'So that, if the fine master Johanan should find you here talking, he... '.

'He would lash us more than he would lash his dogs... '

Peter whistles significantly. Then he says: 'Well it is better if we do this...' and cupping his hands to his mouth he calls out loud: 'Master. Come here. There are some hearts that are suffering and they want You.'

'But what are you saying? Him to come here?! But we are ignoble servants!' The four men are terrified at such boldness.

'But lashes are not pleasant. And if that fine Pharisee should turn up, I would not like to have a share myself...' says Peter, laughing and with his big hand he shakes the most terrified of the four men. Jesus with His long stride is about to arrive. The four men do not know what to do. They would like to run and meet Him but they are paralyzed with respect; poor beings completely frightened by human wickedness, they fall flat on their faces, adoring the Messiah Who is coming towards them.

'Peace to all those who desire Me. Who desires Me, desires good and I love him as a friend. Get up. Who are you? '

But the four just lift their faces off the ground and remain kneeling and quiet.

'They are four servants of the Pharisee Johanan, a relative of Doras.' Peter explains. ' They would like to speak to You, but if he comes, there will be a volley of blows, that is why I said to You: "Come." Get up, boys. He will not eat you! Have faith. Just think that He is a friend of yours.'

'We... we know about You... Jonah told us... '

'I have come for him. I know that he announced Me. What do you know of Me?'

'That You are the Messiah. That he saw You a baby. That the angels sang peace to good people with Your coming, that You were persecuted... that You were saved and that now You have been looking for Your shepherds and... You love them. These last things he told us now. And we thought: if He is so good as to look for some shepherds and love them, He would certainly be also a little fond of

us... We need so much someone who may love us... '
'I love you. Do you suffer much?'
'Oh!... But Doras' men even more. If Johanan found us talking here!... But today he is at Gerghesa. He has not yet come back from the Feast of the Tabernacles. But his steward this evening will give us food after measuring the work that we have done. But it does not matter. We will not rest for our meal at the sixth hour and we will make up for this time.'
'Tell me, man, would I be able to work that implement? Is it a difficult task?' asks Peter.
'No, it's not difficult. But it is hard work. It takes a lot of strength.'
'I have that. Show me. If I succeed, you can talk and I will play the ox. You, John, Andrew and James, come to the lesson. We will abandon fish for the worms of the soil. Come on!' Peter lays his hands on the cross-bar of the beam. There are two men at each plough, one on each side of the long beam. He looks and imitates all the gestures of the peasant. Strong as he is and rested, he works well and the man praises him.
'I am a master in ploughing happily' exclaims good Peter. 'Come on, John! Come here. An ox and a bull-calf at each plough. James and that mute calf of my brother at the other one. Right! Heave away!' and the two ploughs proceed
 side by side turning the soil and cutting furrows in the long field at the end of which they turn round and cut a fresh furrow. They seem to have worked as farmers all their lives.
'How good Your friends are!' says the boldest of Johanan's servants. 'Did You make them such?'
'I have guided their goodness as you do with the pruner's

shears. Goodness was already in them. It now blossoms well because there is Who takes care of it.'

'They are also humble. They are Your friends and yet they are serving us, poor servants, like that! '

'Only those who love humility, meekness, continence, honesty and love, love above all, can stay with Me. Because who loves God and his neighbour, possesses in consequence all virtues and gains Heaven.'

'Shall we be able to gain it, too, we, who have no time to pray, to go to the Temple, not even to raise our heads off the furrows?'

'Tell Me: do you hate him who deals with you so hard? Is there in you rebellion and reproach to God for putting you amongst the lowest of the earth? '

'Oh! no, Master! It is our fate. But when tired we throw ourselves on our pallets, we say: "Well, the God of Abraham knows that we are so exhausted that we are not able to say more than: 'Blessed be the Lord!'", and we also say: "Also today we have lived without sinning"... You know... we could also cheat a little and eat a fruit with our bread, or pour some oil on to the boiled vegetables. But the master said: "Bread and vegetables are sufficient for servants. And at harvest time a little vinegar in the water to quench their thirst and give them strength." And we do that. After all... we could be worse off.'

'And I solemnly tell you that the God of Abraham smiles at your hearts, whilst He turns a severe face towards those who insult Him in the Temple with false prayers, whilst they do not love their fellows.'

'Oh! but they love people like themselves! At least... it looks as if they do because they respect one another with gifts and bows. It is for us that they have no love. But we

are different from them and it is fair.'
'No. It is not fair in My Father's Kingdom. But different will be the way of judging. Not the rich and the mighty ones, as such, will receive honours. But only those who have always loved God, loving Him above themselves and above everything else, such as money, power, women, a bountiful table; and loving their fellow men, that is all men, both rich and poor, well-known and unknown, learned and without culture, good and bad. Yes, you must love also bad people. Not because of their wickedness but out of pity for their souls, which they wound to death. It is necessary to love them imploring the Celestial Father to cure them and redeem them. In the Kingdom of Heaven those will be blessed who have honoured the Lord with truth and justice, who have loved their parents and relatives out of respect; those who have not stolen anything in any way, that is who have given and exacted what is just, also in the work of servants; those who have not killed any reputation or creature and have not desired to kill, even when the behaviour of other people is so cruel as to excite hearts to disdain and rebellion; those who have not sworn falsehood damaging one's neighbour and the truth; those who have not committed adultery or any carnal sin; those, who being mild and resigned, have always accepted their lot without envying others. Of those is the Kingdom of Heaven, also a beggar can be a happy king up there, whereas a Tetrarch, with all his power, will be less than nothing, nay, more than nothing: he will be a prey to Mammon, if he has sinned against the eternal law of the Decalogue.'
The men listen to Him gaping. Near Jesus there are Bartholomew, Matthew, Simon, Philip, Thomas, James and Judas of Alphaeus. The other four continue working,

red in their faces and hot, but cheerful. Peter is quite enough to keep them all merry.

'Oh! How right Jonah was in calling You: "Holy!" Everything is holy in You: Your words, Your look, Your smile. We have never felt our souls thus... ! '

'Have you not seen Jonah for a long time?'

'Since he has been ill.'

'Ill?'

'Yes, Master. He cannot stand it anymore. He was already dragging himself along before. But after the summer work and the vintage he is unable to stand up. And yet that... makes him work... Oh! You say that we must love everybody. But it is very difficult to love hyenas! And Doras is worse than a hyena! '

'Jonah loves him...'

'Yes, Master. And I say that he is a saint like those who have been martyred because of their loyalty to the Lord Our God.'

'You have spoken the truth. What is your name?'

'Micah, and this is Saul, and this is Jowehel, and this is Isaiah.'

'I will mention your names to the Father. And you were saying that Jonah is very ill?'

'Yes, as soon as he finishes his work he throws himself on the straw and we don't see him. The other servants of Doras tell us.'

'Will he be working now?'

'Yes, if he can stand up. He should be beyond that apple orchard.'

'Was Doras' harvest a good one? '

'Yes, it was famous all over the area. The plants had to be propped up owing to the miraculous size of the fruit, and Doras had to have new vats made because there were so

many grapes that the usual ones could not contain them.'
'Doras must have rewarded his servant!'
'Rewarded! Oh! Lord, how little You know of him!'
'But Jonah told Me that years ago Doras thrashed him to death for the loss of a few bunches and that he became a slave through debt because his master blamed him for the loss of a few crops. Since this year he had a miraculous abundance, he should have given him a prize.'
'No. He lashed him savagely, accusing him of not having the same abundance in past years because he had not taken due care of the land.'
'But that man is a beast! 'exclaims Matthew.
'No. He is soulless' says Jesus. 'I leave you, My sons, with a blessing. Have you bread and food for today?'
'We have this bread' and they show Him a dark loaf which they take out of a sack lying on the ground.
'Take My food. I have but this. But I am staying at Doras' today and...'
'You at Doras' house?'
'Yes. To ransom Jonah. Did you not know?'
'No one knows anything here. But... distrust him, Master. You are like a lamb in the wolf's den.'
'He will not be able to do Me any harm. Take My food. James, give them what we have. Also your wine. You must rejoice a little, too, My poor friends. Both your souls and your bodies. Peter! Let us go.'
'I am coming, Master, there is only this furrow to cut.' Then he runs to Jesus, his face drawn with fatigue. He dries himself with the mantle he had taken off, puts it on again and laughs happily. The four men cannot thank them enough.

'Will you pass by here again, Master? '
'Yes. Wait for Me. You will say goodbye to Jonah. Can You do that? '
'Oh! yes. The field is to be ploughed by evening. More than two thirds has been done. How well and quickly. Your friends are strong! May God bless You. Today for us is a greater feast than Passover. Oh! May God bless you all! '

Jesus heads straight to the apple-orchard. They cross it and reach Doras' fields where other peasants are at the ploughs or are bent down removing all the loose weeds from the furrows. But Jonah is not there. The men recognize Jesus and salute Him without leaving their work.
'Where is Jonah?'
'After two hours he fell on the furrow and has been taken home. Poor Jonah. He will not have to suffer long now. He is nearing his end. We shall never have a better friend.'
'You have Me on the earth and him in Abraham's bosom. The dead love the living with a double love: their own and the love they obtain by being with God, therefore a perfect love.'
'Oh! Go to him at once. That he may see You in his suffering!' Jesus blesses and goes away.

'What are You going to do now? What will You say to Doras?' ask the disciples.
'I will go as if I knew nothing. If he sees that he is being met fairly and squarely, he may be pitiless towards Jonah and the servants.'
'Your friend is right; he is a jackal' says Peter to Simon.

'Lazarus speaks nothing but the truth and he is not a backbiter. You will meet him and you will like him' replies Simon.

They see the house of the Pharisee; large, low but well built, country house in the middle of an orchard now fruitless. Peter and Simon go ahead to warn.

Doras comes out. He is old man with the hard profile of a predatory person, with Ironic eyes and a serpent's mouth wriggling a false smile in a beard more white than black.

'Hail, Jesus' he greets informally and with obvious condescension.
'May your salutation return to you' replies Jesus. He does not say "Peace."
'Come in. My house receives You. You have been as punctual as a king.'
'As an honest person' replies Jesus.
Doras laughs as though it were a joke.
Jesus turns round and says to His disciples, who had not been invited: 'Come in. They are My friends.'
'Let them come in... but isn't that one the excise man, the son of Alphaeus? '
'This is Matthew, the disciple of Christ' says Jesus in a tone that the other understands and he gives a laugh more forced than the one before.

Inside, the house is sumptuously rich and comfortable but icy. The servants seem slaves always afraid of punishment and walk with shoulders bent, stealing away swiftly; one feels that the house is dominated by cold-heartedness and hatred.

Doras would like to crush the 'poor' Galilean Master under the wealth of his house which is sumptuous inside. Sumptuous and icy. But Jesus can neither be crushed by a display of wealth nor by a reminder of one's wealth and relatives and Doras, who understands the indifference of the Master, takes Him to his orchard garden, where he shows Him rare plants and offers Him their fruits, which servants bring on golden trays and cups. Jesus enjoys and praises the delicious fruit; beautiful peaches partly in their natural state and partly preserved in an alcoholic syrup, and pears of a rare size. 'I am the only one to have them in Palestine and I don't think that there are any in the whole peninsula. I sent for them to Persia and even farther away. The caravan cost me as much as a talent. But not even the Tetrarchs have such fruits. Perhaps not even Caesar has them. I count all the fruits and I want their stones. And the pears are eaten only at my table because I do not want even one seed to be taken away. I send some to Annas, but only cooked ones so that they are sterile.'
'But they are plants of God. And all men are equal.'
'Equal? No! I equal to... to Your Galileans? '
'Souls come from God and He creates them equal.'
'But I am Doras, the faithful Pharisee!...' says Doras, looking as proud as a peacock. So much taller than Doras, Jesus towers over him, stately in His purple tunic, near the small, slightly bent, wrinkled, Pharisee in a garment strikingly wide and rich in fringes.

After admiring himself for some time, Doras exclaims:' Jesus, why did You send Lazarus, the brother of a prostitute, to the house of Doras, the pure Pharisee? Is Lazarus Your friend? You must not do that. Don't You

know that he is anathematized because his sister Mary is a prostitute?'
'I know but Lazarus and his deeds which are honest.'
'But the world remembers the sin of that house and sees that its stains spread to its friends... Don't go there. Why are You not a Pharisee? If You wish... I am influential... I will have You accepted, although You are a Galilean. I can do anything in the Sanhedrin. Annas is in my hands like the edge of my mantle.
People would be more afraid of You.'
'I want only to be loved.'
'I will love You. You can see that I already love You because I am yielding to Your wish and I am giving You Jonah.'
'I paid for him.'
'True, and I am surprised that You can afford to pay so much.'
'Not I. A friend paid for Me.'
'Well, well. I am not inquisitive. I say: You see that I love You and I want to make You happy. You will have Jonah after our meal. It is only for You that I make this sacrifice...' and he laughs his cruel laughter.
Jesus, with arms folded on His chest, darts more and more severe glances at Doras whilst they remain in the orchard awaiting mealtime.
'But You must make me happy. A joy for a joy. I am giving You my best servant. I am therefore depriving myself of something useful for the future. This year Your blessing- I know that You were here at the beginning of summer- has given me crops that have made my farm famous. Now bless my herds and my fields. Next year I will not regret the loss of Jonah... and in the meantime I will find someone like him. Come and bless. Give me the

joy of being celebrated throughout Palestine and of having folds and granaries full of all sorts of good things. Come' and, overwhelmed by gold-fever, he grasps Jesus and tries to drag Him.
But Jesus resists. 'Where is Jonah?' he asks severely.
'Where they are ploughing. He wanted to do also that for his good master. But before the meal is over he will come. In the meantime, come and bless the herds, the fields, the orchards, the vineyards, the oil mills. Bless everything. Oh! How fruitful they will be next year! Come then.'
'Where is Jonah?' asks Jesus in a louder thundering voice.
'I told You! Where they are ploughing. He is the first servant and does not work: he is at the head of the men.'
'Liar! '
'Me? I swear to it by Jehovah!'
'Perjurer!'
'Me? I a perjurer? I am the most faithful believer! Watch how You speak!'
'Killer!' Jesus has been raising His voice louder and louder and this last word is like thunder. His disciples go near Him, servants peep out of doors frightened. Jesus' face is unendurable in its severity and phosphorescent rays seem to emanate from His eyes.
For a moment, Doras is frightened and shrinks; a bundle of fine cloth near the tall person of Jesus, clad in a dark red woollen tunic. Then Doras' pride prevails and he shouts with a voice, squeaky like a fox's:
'Only I give orders in my house. Get out, vile Galilean.'
'I will go out after I curse you, your fields, herds and vineyards for this year and the years to come.'
'No, don't! Yes. It is true. Jonah is ill. But he is being

taken care of. He is well looked after. Withdraw Your curse.'
'Where is Jonah? Let a servant lead Me to him at once. I paid for him; and since he is a piece of merchandise, a machine, for you, I consider him as such; and since I purchased him, I want him.'
Doras pulls out a gold whistle from his chest and blows it three times. A group of servants, both of the house and of the fields, emerge from everywhere and run to the dreaded master, bowing so deeply, that they seem to be crawling.
'Bring Jonah to Him and hand him over....Where are You going?'
Jesus does not answer but follows the servants who have rushed beyond the garden towards the filthy holes that are the poor peasants' dwellings.

They enter Jonah's hovel where Jonah, now only skin and bones and panting because of a high temperature, is lying half naked on a cane mat with only a patched up garment for a mattress and an even more worn out mantle for a blanket, being looked after by Mary, the wife of his friend, the same Mary who had nursed him when Doras had thrashed him almost to dead.
'Jonah! My friend! I have come to take you away!'
'You? My Lord! I am dying... but I am happy to have You here!'
'My faithful friend, you are now free and you will not die here. I am taking you to My house.'
'Free? Why? To Your house? Oh! Yes. You did promise me that I would see Your Mother.'
Jesus bends lovingly over the miserable bed of the unhappy man and Jonah, account of his joy, seems to

revive.
'Peter, you are strong. Lift up Jonah. And you, give your mantles. This bed is too hard for one in his state.'
The disciples take off their mantles at once, fold them several times and lay them on the mat, using some as a pillow. Peter lays down his load of bones and Jesus covers him with His own mantle.
'Peter, have you got any money? '
'Yes, Master, I have forty coins.'
'Good. Let us go. Cheer up, Jonah. A little more trouble and then there will be so much peace in My house, near Mary...'
'Mary... yes... oh! Your house!' And in his extreme weakness poor Jonah does the only thing he can do; he weeps.
'Goodbye, woman. The Lord will bless you for your mercy.'
'Goodbye, Lord. Goodbye, Jonah. Pray for me.' says the young woman, weeping.

Doras appears when they reach the door and frightened, Jonah covers his face. But Jesus lays a hand on his head and goes out beside him, sterner than a judge. The unhappy procession goes out into the rustic yard and takes the path in the orchard.
'That bed is mine! I sold You the servant, not the bed.'
Jesus throws the purse at his feet without saying a word. Doras picks up the purse and empties it. 'Forty coins and five didrachmas. It's too little!'
Jesus looks the greedy revolting torturer up and down but gives no reply.
'At least tell me that You are withdrawing the anathema!'
But with a glare and a few words, Jesus crushes him

once again; 'I entrust you to the God of Sinai' and walks past, upright, beside the rustic litter, that Peter and Andrew are carrying most cautiously.

When Doras sees that it is all to no good, that the punishment is certain, he shouts: 'We will meet again, Jesus! I will have You in my clutches again! I will fight You to death. You can take that worn out man. I no longer need him. I will save his burial money. Go, go away, cursed Satan! I will set the whole Sanhedrin on You. Satan! Satan!'

Jesus feigns that He does not hear but the disciples are dismayed. Attending only to Jonah, Jesus looks for the smoothest and the most sheltered paths until they reach a crossroad near Jonathan's field.

The four peasants run to say goodbye to their friend who is leaving and to Jesus Who is blessing.

But the road from Esdraelon to Nazareth is long and their speed slow because of their pitiful load. Along the main road, there is neither wagon nor cart and they proceed in silence, with Jonah seemingly asleep but also holding on to the hand of Jesus.

As evening falls, it starts to and a covered Roman military wagon with two or three soldiers, catches up with them.

'In the name of God, stop' says Jesus lifting His arm. The soldiers stop and a pompous looking non-commissioned officer peeps out from underneath the cover.

'What do You want?' he asks Jesus.

'I have a dying friend. I ask you to take him into the wagon.

'We are not allowed... but... get on. We are not dogs either.'

They lift the litter into the wagon.
'Your friend? Who are You?'
'Rabbi Jesus of Nazareth.'
'You? Oh!...' The non-commissioned officer looks at Him curiously.
'If it is You, then... get on as many as you can. But don't let anyone see you... It is an order... but above orders there is also humanity, isn't there? You are good, I know. Eh! We soldiers know everything... How do I know? Even stones speak well or evil and we have ears to listen to them in order to serve Caesar. You are not a false Christ like the others before You, who were agitators and rebels. You are good. Rome knows. This man... is very ill.'
'That is why I am taking him to My Mother.'
'Hum! She won't cure him for long! Give him some wine. It's in that canteen. Aquila, whip the horses. Quintus, give me the ration of honey and butter. It's mine. It will do him good; he has a cough and honey will help.'
'You are good.'
'No. Not quite so bad as many. And I am happy to have You here with me. Remember Publius Quintilianus of the Italica legion. I stay at Caesarea. But I am now going to Ptolomais. Inspection order.'
'You are not My enemy.'
'I? I am an enemy of bad people. Never of good people. And I would like to be good, too. Tell me: What doctrine do You preach for us, military people?'
'The doctrine is one only for everybody. Justice, honesty, continence, compassion. One must do one's duty without any abuses. Also in the hard necessities of the army, one must be human. And one must endeavour to know the Truth, that is; God, one and eternal, without which knowledge every action is deprived of grace and

consequently of eternal reward.'
'But when I am dead, what will I do with the good I have done?'
'Who comes to the true God will find that good in the next life.'
'Am I going to be born again? Will I become a tribune or even an emperor? '
'No. You will become like God, being united to His eternal beatitude in Heaven.'
'What? Me in Olympus? Amongst the gods? '
'There are no gods. There is the true God. The One I preach. The One Who hears you and notes your goodness and your desire to know the Good.'
'I like that! I did not know that God could be concerned with a poor heathen soldier.'
'He created you, Publius. He therefore loves you and would like to have you with Himself.'
'Eh!... why not? But... no one ever speaks to us of God.'
'I will come to Caesarea and you will hear Me.'
'Oh! Yes. I will come to hear You. There is Nazareth. I would like to serve You further. But if they see me... '
'I will get off and I bless you for your kindness.'
'Hail, Master.'
'May the Lord show Himself to you, soldiers. Goodbye.'
They get off and resume walking.
'In a short while you will be able to rest, Jonah' says Jesus encouragingly.

Jonah smiles. As night falls, he grows calmer and calmer now that he is sure that he is far from Doras. John and his brother run ahead to inform Mary. When the little procession arrives in Nazareth, now almost deserted in the late evening, Mary is already at the door awaiting Her Son.

'Mother, here is Jonah. He is taking shelter under Your kindness to begin enjoying his Paradise. Are you happy, Jonah? '
'Happy! Happy!' whispers the exhausted man as one who is in ecstasy. They take him into the little room where Joseph died.
'You are in My father's bed. And here is My Mother and I am here. See? Nazareth becomes Bethlehem and you are now the little Jesus between two people who love you. And these are the ones who venerate you as the faithful servant. You cannot see the angels but they are waving their bright wings above you and singing the words of the Christmas psalm...'
Jesus pours all His kindness on poor Jonah who is deteriorating from one second to the next. He seems to have resisted so far in order to die here... but he is happy. He smiles and tries to kiss Jesus' hand and Mary's, and to say... but his anguish interrupts his words. Mary comforts him like a mother. And he repeats: 'Yes... yes' with a blissful smile on his emaciated face. The disciples, standing at the kitchen garden entranced, are silent and watch, deeply moved.
'God has listened to your long desire. The Star of your long night is now becoming the Star of your eternal Morning. You know its name' says Jesus.
'Jesus, Yours! Oh! Jesus! The angels... Who will sing the angelical hymn for me? My soul can hear it... but also my ears wish to hear it... Who?... to make me sleep happy... I am so sleepy! So much work I have done! So many tears... So many insults... Doras... I forgive him... but I do not want to hear his voice and I hear it. It is like the voice of Satan near me, who am dying. Who will cover that voice for me with the words that came from Heaven?'

It is Mary Who on the same tune as Her lullaby sings softly: 'Glory to God in the Highest Heaven and peace to men down here.' And She repeats it two or three times because She sees that Jonah calms down on hearing it. 'Doras does not speak any more' Jonah says after some time. 'Only the angels... It was a Child... in a manger... between an ox and a donkey... and it was the Messiah... And I adored Him... and with Him there was Joseph and Mary...' His voice fades away in a short gurgle and then there is silence.

'Peace in Heaven to the man of good will! He is dead. We shall bury him in our poor sepulchre. He deserves to await the resurrection of the dead near My just father' says Jesus just as Mary of Alphaeus comes in.

Jesus In The House Of Lazarus. Martha Speaks Of The Magdalene

It is the market square in Jericho with its trees, shouting vendors and in the corner, there's Zacchaeus, the tax collector, intent on his legal and illegal extortions; dealing also in jewellery and other valuables, which he weighs and appraises in payment of taxes or in exchange for other goods. It is now the turn of a slender woman who is completely clad in a huge rust-grey mantle and her face hidden beneath a yellowish closely woven byssus*. only the slimness of her figure can be seen notwithstanding the huge greyish cloak that envelops her. But what little can be seen of her says she is a young woman; her feet, shod in rather sophisticated sandals fitted with uppers and interlacing leather straps so that only her smooth juvenile toes and part of her slim white ankles are visible and her hand, which, for a moment, she takes out from beneath the mantle to hand over a bracelet without saying a word, takes the money without objection and turns round to go away.

* a fine textile fibre and fabric of flax

Behind her, Judas Iscariot watches her carefully and when she makes to depart, he says a word to her but she makes no reply, as if she were dumb, and hastens away in her mass of clothes.

'Who is she?' Judas asks Zacchaeus.

'I do not ask my customers their names, especially when they are as kind as she is.'

'Young, isn't she?'

'Apparently.'

'Is she Judaean?'

'Who knows?! Gold is yellow in all countries.'

'Show me that bracelet.'

'Do you want to buy it?'

'No.'

'Well, nothing doing. What do you think? That it will start talking in her place?'

'I wanted to see if I could find out who she is...'

'Are you so interested? Are you a necromancer who divines, or a bloodhound that scents? Go away, forget her. If she is like that, she is either honest and unhappy or she is a leper. Therefore... nothing doing.'

'I am not craving for a woman' replies Judas contemptuously.

'May be... but by the looks of your face I can hardly believe it. Well, if you do not want anything else, please step aside. I have other people to attend to.'

Judas turns away angry and asks a bread vendor and a fruit seller whether they know the woman who had just bought some bread and apples from them, and whether they know where she lives.

'She has been coming here for some time, every two or three days. But we do not know where she lives.' they reply.

'But how does she speak?' insists Judas. The two laugh

and reply: 'With her tongue.'
Judas abuses them and goes away... and runs into the group of Jesus and His disciples, who have come to buy some bread and food for their daily meal. The surprise is reciprocal and... not very enthusiastic. Jesus says only: 'You are here?' says Jesus, simply.
Judas mumbles something, Peter breaks into a loud laugh and says: 'Here, I am blind and a misbeliever. I cannot see the vineyards. And I don't believe in the miracle...'
'What are you saying?' ask two or three disciples.
'I am speaking the truth. There are no vineyards here. And I cannot believe that Judas, in all this dust, can gather grapes simply because he is a disciple of the Rabbi.'
'Vintage finished a long time ago' replies Judas harshly.
'And Kerioth is many miles away' concludes Peter.
'You are attacking me at once. You are hostile to me.'
'No. I am not such a fool as you think.'
'That is enough' commands Jesus, severe. Then He addresses Judas: 'I was not expecting to see you here. I thought you would be in Jerusalem for the Tabernacles.'
'I am going there tomorrow. I have been waiting here for a friend of our family, who...'
'Please, that is enough.'
'Do You not believe me, Master? I swear...'
'I did not ask you anything and please do not say anything. You are here. That is enough. Are you thinking of coming with us or have you still got business to attend to? Answer frankly.'
'No... I have finished. In any case that fellow is not coming and I am going to Jerusalem for the Feast. And where are You going?'

'To Jerusalem.'
'Today?'
'I will be at Bethany this evening.'
'At Lazarus' house? '
'Yes, at Lazarus'.'
'Well, I will come too.'
'Yes, come as far as Bethany. Then Andrew with James of Zebedee and Thomas will go to Gethsemane to make preparations and wait for us all and you will go with them.' says Jesus, stressing the last words so that Judas does not react.
'And what about us?' asks Peter.
'You will go with My cousins and Matthew where I will send you and will come back in the evening. John, Simon, Bartholomew and Philip will stay with Me, that is, they will go and announce in Bethany that the Rabbi has come and will speak to the people at the ninth hour.'
They walk quickly across the barren countryside, conscious of an impending storm, not in the clear sky but in their hearts and they proceed silently.

Lazarus' house is one of the first houses upon arrival in Bethany from Jericho.
When they reach Bethany, Jesus dismisses the group that is to go to Jerusalem (Gethsemane). Then He sends the second group towards Bethlehem saying:
 'Go and do not worry. Half way you will find Isaac, Elias, and the others. Tell them that I will be in Jerusalem for many days and I expect them to bless them.'

Simon, in the meantime, has knocked at the door and had it opened. The servants inform Lazarus who comes at once. Judas Iscariot, who had gone a few yards ahead,

returns with the excuse of saying to Jesus: 'I have displeased You, Master. I realize it. Forgive me' whilst at the same time, through the open gate, he casts sidelong glances at the garden and at the house.
'Yes. It is all right. Go. Do not keep your companions waiting.' And Judas must go.
'He was hoping there might be a change in the instructions.' Peter whispers
'Never, Peter. I know what I am doing. But bear with that man...'
'I will try. But I cannot promise... Goodbye, Master. Come, Matthew and you two. Quick.'
'My peace be always with you.'

Jesus goes in with the remaining four. He kisses Lazarus, introduces John, Philip and Bartholomew and then dismisses them and remains alone with Lazarus.
They go towards the house, where, beneath the beautiful porch, is a woman; Martha is swarthy and tall, though not quite so tall as her fair-haired, rosy sister. But she is a beautiful young woman with a well-shaped, balanced, plump body, a small dark head with a smooth brown forehead. Her mild, dark, long-shaped eyes are kind and as soft as velvet, between dark eyelashes. Her nose is slightly turned down and her small lips very red against her dark cheeks. She smiles showing strong snow-white teeth.
Her dark blue woollen dress has red and dark green trimming around the neck and at the end of the wide short sleeves, from which two other sleeves unfold, of very fine white linen, tied and pleated at the wrists by a little cord.
Her very fine white blouse shows also at the top of her

breast and around the lower part of her neck where it is held tight by a cord. A blue, red and green scarf of fine cloth serves as a belt, tied around the upper part of her hips and hangs down her left side in a tuft of fringes. Her dress is rich and chaste.

'I have a sister, Master. Here she is, Martha. She is good and pious, the consolation and the honour of the family and the joy of poor Lazarus. Before she was my first and only joy. Now she is the second because You are the first.'
Martha prostrates herself on the floor and kisses the hem of Jesus' tunic.
'Peace to the good sister and to the chaste woman. Stand up.'
Martha rises to her feet and enters the house with Jesus and Lazarus. Then she asks for leave to attend to the house.
'She is my peace...'whispers Lazarus, looking at Jesus, an inquisitive look, but Jesus pretends He does not see it.
'And Jonah? ' Lazarus asks
'He is dead.'
'Dead? Then...'
'I got him when he was dying. But he died a free man and happy in My house, at Nazareth, between Me and My Mother.'
'Doras practically killed him for You before handing him over! '
'Yes, with fatigue and also with blows.'
'He is a devil and hates You. That hyena hates the whole world... Did he not tell You that he hates You?'
'Yes, he did.'
'Distrust him, Jesus. He is capable of anything, Lord...

what did Doras tell You? Did he not tell You to shun me? Did he not place poor Lazarus in a disgraceful light? '
'I think that you know Me well enough to understand that I judge for Myself and according to justice and that when I love, I love without considering whether such love may procure Me good or evil according to the views of the world.'
'But that man is cruel and he injures and hurts severely... He tormented me also some days ago. He came here and he told me... Oh! I am so vexed already! Why does he want to take You also away from me?'
'I am the solace of those who are tormented and the companion of those who are forlorn. I have come to you also for that..'
'Ah! Then You know?... Oh! shame on me!'
'No. Why on you? I know. So what? Shall I anathematise you, who are suffering? I am Mercy, Peace, Forgiveness, Love for everybody; and what shall I be for those who are innocent? The sin for which you suffer is not yours. Shall I be pitiless towards you if I feel pity also for her?...'
'Have You seen her?'
'I have. Do not cry.'
But Lazarus, his head resting on his folded arms on the table, is weeping, sobbing painfully.
Martha appears at the door and looks in. Jesus nods to her to be silent. And Martha goes away with big tears running silently down her cheeks.
Slowly, Lazarus calms down and apologises for his weakness. Jesus comforts him and as His friend wishes to withdraw for a moment, He goes out into the garden and walks among the flowerbeds, where some purple roses are still in bloom.
Martha joins Him shortly afterwards.

'Master, has Lazarus spoken to You?'
'Yes, Martha, he has.'
'Lazarus cannot set his mind at rest since he is aware that You know and that You have seen her...'
'How does he know?'
'First, that man who was with You and says he is Your disciple: the young one, tall, swarthy, clean-shaven... then Doras. Doras lashed You with his contempt, the disciple only said that You had seen her on the lake... with her lovers... '
'Do not cry for that! Do you think that I am unacquainted with your wound? I was aware of it since I was with the Father... Do not lose heart, Martha. Raise your heart and your head.'
'Pray for her, Master. I pray... but I cannot forgive completely and perhaps the Eternal Father rejects my prayer.'
'You are right: you must forgive to be forgiven and heard. I already pray for her. But give Me your forgiveness and Lazarus'. You, a good sister, can speak and achieve even more than I can. His wound is too fresh and sore for My hand to touch it even lightly. You can do it. Give Me your full holy forgiveness, and I will... '
'Forgive... We will not be able. Our mother died of grief through her ill deeds and... they were still slight compared with the present ones. I see my mother's torture... it is always present to me. And I see what Lazarus is suffering.'
'She is ill, Martha, and insane. Forgive her.'
'She is possessed, Master.'
'And what is diabolic possession but a disease of the spirit infected by Satan to the extent that it degenerates into a diabolic spiritual being? How can certain

perversions in human beings be explained otherwise? Perversions that make man fiercer than beasts, more lewd than monkeys and so on and make a hybrid, in which man, animal and demon are mingled. That is the explanation of what amazes us as an inexplicable monstrosity in so many creatures. Do not weep. Forgive. I see. Because My sight is sharper than the sight of the eye or of the heart. I see God. I see. I tell you: forgive, because she is ill.'

'Cure her, then! '

'I will cure her. Have faith. I will make you happy. But forgive and tell Lazarus to forgive. Forgive her. Love her. Be on familiar terms with her. Speak to her as if she were like you. Speak to her of Me... '

'How do You expect her to understand You, the Holy One?'

'She may not seem to understand. But My Name, even by Itself, is salvation. Get her to think of Me and to mention My Name. Oh! Satan runs away when a heart thinks of My Name. Smile, Martha, at this hope. Look at this rose; the rain of the past days had spoiled it but look, the sun today has opened it and it is even more beautiful because the drops of rain on the petals adorn it with diamonds. Your house will be like that... Tears and sorrow, now, and later...joy and glory. Go! Tell Lazarus, while I, in the peace of Your garden, will pray the Father for Mary and for you... '

END

www.ingramcontent.com/pod-product-compliance
Lightning Source LLC
Chambersburg PA
CBHW061330040426
42444CB00011B/2851